Paths
of the
Past

TENNESSEE THREE STAR BOOKS

Paths of the Past

Tennessee, 1770–1970

BY PAUL H. BERGERON

PUBLISHED IN COOPERATION WITH

The Tennessee Historical Commission

THE UNIVERSITY OF TENNESSEE PRESS

KNOXVILLE

TENNESSEE THREE STAR BOOKS / *Paul H. Bergeron, General Editor*

This series of general-interest books about significant Tennessee topics is sponsored jointly by the Tennessee Historical Commission and the University of Tennessee Press. Inquiries about manuscripts should be addressed to Professor Bergeron, History Department, University of Tennessee, Knoxville. Orders and questions concerning titles in the series should be addressed to the University of Tennessee Press, Knoxville, 37996-0325.

Manufactured in the United States of America.

Cloth: 1st printing, 1979; 2nd printing, 1988.
Paper: 1st printing, 1979; 2nd printing, 1981;
3rd printing, 1988; 4th printing, 1992.

The paper in this book meets the minimum requirements of the American National Standard for Permanence of Paper for Printed Library Materials. ♾ The binding materials have been chosen for strength and durability.

Library of Congress Cataloging in Publication Data

Bergeron, Paul H. 1938–
Paths of the past: Tennessee, 1770–1970.
(Tennessee three star books)
Bibliography: p.
Includes index.
1. Tennessee—History. I. Title. II. Series.
F436.B47 976.8 79–14896
ISBN 0–87049–283–7 (cloth: alk. paper)
ISBN 0–87049–274–8 (pbk.: alk. paper)

ABOUT THE AUTHOR

Paul H. Bergeron is professor of history at the University of Tennessee, Knoxville, where he has been a member of the faculty since 1972. In 1987 he was appointed Editor of the Andrew Johnson Papers. His major publications include: Volumes 1 and 2 of the *Correspondence of James K. Polk* (wth Herbert Weaver); *Antebellum Politics in Tennessee;* and *The Presidency of James K. Polk.*

Cover Photograph: The Dean Cornwell mural in the State Office Building reproduced courtesy of the Tennessee Tourism Development Division.

To my sons, Pierre, André, and Louis.

All Tennessee-born,

they are my "three-star series."

Preface

To attempt a brief summary of two centuries of Tennessee's history is to embark upon a nearly impossible assignment, for the task necessarily imposes upon the author the burden of selectivity. Nevertheless, it has been exciting, as well as frustrating, to pick and choose topics from among Tennessee's very rich past. Doubtless in the eyes of some readers and critics my decisions to include certain things, while excluding others, may seem ill-advised, if not capricious. I hope, however, that most readers will conclude that I have chosen well and thus have represented the state's history in a fair and interesting manner.

I would not have undertaken this tremendous responsibility had it not been for the encouragement and urging of Louis T. Iglehart, recently retired director of the University of Tennessee Press, and LeRoy P. Graf, head of the history department at the University in Knoxville. Their faith in me as the person to write this summary history surely must have wavered from time to time, but they never let me know it. In the final phase of manuscript revision, Mr. Iglehart assisted me in a masterful and conscientious way, for which I am very grateful.

Since the fall of 1972, I have had the opportunity to teach Tennessee history at the University of Tennessee, Knoxville. Were it not for this particular challenge over the past several years, I would not have felt the least bit prepared for the responsibility of producing a concise history of the state. I am therefore indebted to my students who have tolerantly, and sometimes enthusiastically, listened to my efforts to reveal and interpret the state's past and have unknowingly guided me in various ways. Good naturedly they have permitted a non-native Tennessean to tell them about their state—warts and all.

Like any historian who attempts a general history of a state or region, I have stood upon the shoulders of scholars and well-informed amateur historians whose writings have preceded mine. Perceptive readers of my study will recognize material that I have borrowed from other students of Tennessee's past. To the whole company of authors who have made Tennessee the object of their inquiry and publication, I am most appreciative.

In a very real sense, this manuscript would never have reached the publisher had it not been for the secretaries in the History Department who cheerfully typed and retyped versions of it. I especially wish to single out Mrs. Linda Parrish, who has done yeoman service in this regard.

Finally, I confess that the unfailing aid and support of my wife, Mary Lee, has been responsible for seeing this project through to its completion. This she has done while following her own professional career and caring for our three young sons.

PAUL H. BERGERON

April 1979
Knoxville, Tennessee

Contents

ILLUSTRATIONS

Paths of the Past

Introduction

What's in a name? Would Tennessee still be the same if it were known by a different name? Perhaps. What does the name Tennessee mean? No one knows for certain. It is of Cherokee origin, for one of the towns in the Overhill settlements bore that name. Legend has it that at the constitutional convention in 1796 Andrew Jackson proposed the name Tennessee, but the historical record is silent on this point. Actually, early maps of the region that antedate statehood usually labelled the area Tennessee, indicating that the name had been in use for some time before the framers set about to devise a constitution and to name a new state. The mystery surrounding the state's name and how it came to be chosen calls to mind the realization that there are a number of unexplainable aspects of the region and its history. Why, for example, does the Tennessee River flow north through West Tennessee instead of heading southwest to the Gulf of Mexico or why does a perpetual haze seem to enshroud the Great Smoky Mountains?

That the state carries an Indian name serves as a lasting reminder of the significance of Indians in Tennessee's history—until about 1840. The area was Indian country for generations, even centuries, before whites began establishing permanent settlements in the late 1760s and early 1770s. From about the mid-eighteenth century, however, the Cherokees were the only tribe actually to reside in Tennessee, although others claimed portions of Tennessee as their hunting grounds. The Chickasaws in fact held onto their claim of all of present-day West Tennessee until 1818, when Jackson helped to arrange the purchase of that vast tract. One simply cannot tell the story of Tennessee during the half century after 1770 without giving attention to the Indians and their struggles with whites.

Visitors to the state in the 1960s must have been puzzled by the signs welcoming them to the "three states of Tennessee." There is probably not another state in the entire nation that is so clearly divided into three sections or that has felt the impact of intrastate sectionalism to the degree that Tennessee has. Predestined by the forces of geography, Tennessee has been a region of distinct sections (frequently called "Grand Divisions") for at least as long as the two hundred years of white settlement. East Tennessee—the region of Cherokees and of the initial white communities—extends from the lofty heights of the Unaka Mountains westward to the Cumberland Plateau. Stretching from the Cumberland Plateau on the east all the way to the Tennessee River on the west is Middle Tennessee—the state's largest section and in some respects its dominant one. Across the Tennessee River west to the Mississippi is found the much flatter land of West Tennessee—a heavily agricultural region which paradoxically contains the state's largest city, Memphis.

What geography originally did, man continued. From the early beginnings of white penetration of the Tennessee country, sectional differences arose—such as conflicting attitudes toward the parent state, North Carolina; differing agricultural activities; and the less advanced political and economic development of the middle part of the Tennessee region in those days. Gradually over time, political and governmental leaders, and plain folk as well, began to acknowledge sectional divisions. Such recognition soon appeared in the state's laws and constitutions. That Tennessee had no permanent capital city until nearly fifty years after achieving statehood—Knoxville, Nashville, and Murfreesboro were among the early temporary seats of government—indicates the enduring stresses and tensions of competing sections within the state. Sectional rivalry reached new heights when the Civil War crisis arrived. East Tennessee voted against secession from the Union and refused to support the Confederacy during the war years. These developments insured that for decades afterwards the eastern third of the state would be viewed by Middle and West Tennessee as something of an outcast. While improved transportation and communication in the twentieth century have diminished intrastate sectionalism, it nevertheless remains a reality of political, economic, and cultural life. No wonder that state officials in the 1960s decided to advertise the "three states of Tennessee." But such a public announcement of Tennessee's internal rivalries apparently embarrassed and troubled some governmental leaders, for in the early 1970s the welcoming signs were changed. Travelers are now greeted to the "great state of Tennessee."

As the succeeding chapters show, black Tennesseans were an integral part of Tennessee's sections almost from the beginning. Invariably whites took their black slaves with them to the new regions. And together, white and black, they contended against an untamed wilderness and a resentful red people. Twenty years after the founding of permanent white settlements, there were 3,400 slaves in the Southwest Territory, the area that is now Tennessee. By 1860 that figure had swelled to approximately 276,000 (or 25 percent of the state's inhabitants). In the early twentieth century, blacks began leaving the rural areas in appreciable numbers, so that by 1930 half of the black population was living in cities (the state as a whole did not reach that level of urbanization until thirty years later). In addition, the number of blacks throughout Tennessee began to decline in relation to the state's total population, and by 1970 blacks accounted for slightly under 16 percent of Tennessee's residents. These statistics, of course, tell only a small segment of the story of black Tennesseans. Their activities, difficulties, and accomplishments —as they moved from slavery to quasi-freedom to real freedom—are discussed in the following pages.

Tennessee's experiences with its black population are a reminder that the state was and is Southern—but how Southern? Hardly a more tantalizing and difficult question could be raised about the state. Tennessee's geographical location naturally causes the state to be considered as a Border South state. Thus, it is argued, Tennessee has more in common with Kentucky and Missouri, for example, than with Mississippi and Alabama. Touched by parts of eight different states—Arkansas, Missouri, Kentucky, Virginia, North Carolina, Georgia, Alabama, and Mississippi —Tennessee has been influenced in numerous ways by these neighbors. As the subsequent chapters indicate, from time to time Tennessee seemed to identify mainly with the Deep South states that lay along its boundaries, yet at other times and situations Tennessee displayed a more "Northern" orientation. Hence the Border (or Upper) South label is more than a matter of geographical location. Furthermore, the Border South designation can be misleading unless qualified, for it does not take account of Tennessee's sectional differences. Thus, anyone attempting to amplify or explain the label must first ask which part of Tennessee was and is more Southern than the other parts of the state. And that question, in turn, leads to another: at what point did it become so? Although difficult to answer and frustrating in their riddle-like quality, such questions serve as an invitation to delve into the unique features of Tennessee's past.

The images evoked by the name Tennessee might be equally misleading, if taken singly. Some persons might conjure up a vision of plantation life—fields of cotton with blacks tilling the soil and well-to-do whites enjoying life in columned mansions. There was some of this life in Tennessee's antebellum experience, certainly, but it could not be called truly representative of the state. Other individuals might emphasize the perilous but exhilarating days of early white settlement in which pioneers carved out space in a vast wilderness, fought the Indians, and cheered the heroic exploits of John Sevier and James Robertson. This history, too, is a vital part of Tennessee's heritage, although the image would be incomplete without inclusion also of hungry land speculators and other less romantic aspects of late eighteenth-century life. To still others, the name Tennessee stirs notions of more modern developments, such as TVA and the installations at Oak Ridge. The work of TVA and the activities at Oak Ridge have exerted a tremendous impact on Tennessee for at least forty years, but this image, too, is incomplete—still evolving and representing only a brief period in the state's recent past. To a great many non-Tennessee residents, of course, mention of the state brings forth images of country music in Nashville, blues in Memphis, and hillbilly bands in Knoxville. And students of national political history naturally think first of the three controversial, fiercely independent Presidents from Tennessee—Andrew Jackson, James K. Polk, and Andrew Johnson.

Simply to make mention of these diverse images and notions about Tennessee—the list is by no means exhausted here—is to indicate the richness and variety of the state's past. The summary history which follows attempts to present an enticing array of the images and realities of Tennessee's historical dimension.

1. From Frontier to Statehood, 1770–1820

In 1770 white men came to the Tennessee country to stay. Across the mountains and down the rivers and valleys of what is now East Tennessee, the pioneers quickly moved to establish permanent settlements in a vast and alluring wilderness. With a total population of about one hundred sturdy frontier folk, communities sprang up at Watauga (in the vicinity of present-day Elizabethton), Nolichucky (near present-day Erwin), Carter's Valley (in the Rogersville area) and North Holston (in the Kingsport-Bristol area). A half century later a dramatic transformation had taken place, for by 1820 some 423,000 persons dwelled in a land stretching from the Unaka Mountains to the Mississippi River. The days of rough-hewn pioneer life had almost entirely disappeared in a state increasingly populated and "civilized." Packed into the fifty-year story are fascinating political, economic, and social developments that give eloquent testimony of the determination of the people to subdue the Indians, tame the land, and eventually prevail over innumerable obstacles.

The decade of the 1770s—the Watauga years—represents the first step in the evolution from frontier to statehood. An almost unrelenting stream of pioneers ventured forth into the Tennessee country from the neighboring areas of Virginia and North Carolina after the Indian Treaty of Lochaber (1770) granted permission, so the settlers thought, to white occupation of the region. Some undoubtedly left their homes for the Tennessee wilderness simply because they welcomed the excitement and challenge of the unknown, while the lure of new and abundant land most certainly acted as a magnet upon others. Furthermore, some members of the North Carolina "Regulator" group pushed into the west after their final defeat in 1771. The Regulators were residents of the North Carolina backcountry, who harbored numerous grievances about taxation, unrepresentative local governments, exorbitant fees of court officials and lawyers, and problems over acquiring titles to their lands. The colonial government of North Carolina prevailed over the Regulators' protests, however, eventually defeating the dissenters in a pitched battle. Although the actual number of Regulators who moved into the Tennessee region is debatable, there is no doubt that a sizable group traveled across the mountains. In sum, a variety of motives compelled brave souls to congregate in upper East Tennessee in the 1770s.

Of the original four settlements, only one—the North Holston—was located outside Cherokee lands. Thus, after the Lochaber treaty lines were surveyed in 1771, British officials responsible for Indian affairs in the southern colonies ordered the settlers of the other three—Watauga, Nolichucky, and Carter's Valley—to evacuate their newly established homes. In response to this command and in recognition of their precarious existence beyond the protection of either Virginia or North Carolina, the three communities banded together as the Watauga Association in the spring of 1772. The wilderness government they hoped to create was spelled out in the Watauga Compact.

Years ago Donald Davidson wrote that the major problem confronting the early Tennessee settlers was what to do with the Cherokees. He might have added, of course, that the main difficulty facing the Cherokees was what to do with the white intruders. Shortly after the creation of the Watauga Association, an emissary went to the Cherokee towns on the Little Tennessee River to arrange a treaty by which the white settlers would *lease* their lands from the Indians. This arrangement worked quite well for nearly three years, during which time the population at the white settlements increased steadily. In March of 1775, Judge Richard Henderson of North Carolina met with the Cherokees at Sycamore Shoals (site of present-day Elizabethton) and devised a treaty whereby his Transylvania Company purchased two immense tracts of land: one included almost all of present-day Kentucky and the other encompassed most of Middle Tennessee. The only Cherokee voice raised in protest against the Sycamore Shoals treaty was that of Dragging Canoe, son of a highly respected Cherokee chief. For the moment, however, his warnings about the encroachment of whites went unheeded. After Henderson's unabashed display of greed, the Wataugans boldly approached the Cherokees with a proposal of their own: they wanted to *buy* the lands they had previously leased in East Tennessee. With little fanfare but much alacrity, the bargain was struck.

A year later, however, the amicable arrangements between the Cherokees and the Wataugans collapsed when Dragging Canoe and other militant Cherokees directed an attack upon the white settlements. The Wataugans quickly turned back the Cherokee offensive of July 1776. And in September, Virginia and North Carolina troops, as well as Wataugan fighters, launched a counterattack upon the Indians. Nearly two thousand strong, the frontier army moved unimpeded to the Cherokee towns on the Little Tennessee River and burned several of them in retaliation.

But before these events had developed, various Watauga leaders decided that since the American Revolution had begun, they must get under the protective wing of either Virginia or North Carolina. Accordingly, on July 5, 1776 (the day after the thirteen colonies declared their independence) the Watauga settlers petitioned North Carolina for annexation. In due course the document was received by North Carolina's new provisional government which, in turn, directed the Tennessee leaders to select representatives to send to the constitutional convention in November. When the time came, four Watauga delegates crossed the mountains, participated in the convention, and signed the new state constitution. A few months later, in 1777, North Carolina established Washington County, which included most of present-day Tennessee. By this action the Watauga Association thus went out of existence.

In the winter and spring of 1779–80 approximately three hundred hardy pioneers migrated to the Cumberland River basin area of Middle Tennessee, more than two hundred miles to the west by direct land route. The instigator of this hazardous movement of people from one wilderness region to an even more isolated one was none other than Judge Richard Henderson, still hoping to capitalize on his 1775 purchase of the Middle Tennessee tract. He enlisted James Robertson, a leader of the Watauga settlements, to undertake direction and supervision of this venture. Perhaps Robertson, like numerous other frontier settlers, was simply not content to remain in one spot for long and welcomed the challenge of moving west. Stories of the fertile basin of Middle Tennessee merely added incentive to seek fame and fortune there. After Robertson agreed to accept Henderson's proposition, he then convinced John Donelson, a resident of southwestern Virginia, to take charge of the group that was to travel by water.

Robertson first led an exploring party to the Cumberland Basin to reconnoiter the region and make plans for the subsequent migration. They went from upper East Tennessee into Kentucky, via the Cumberland Gap, and followed a path that closely paralleled the Cumberland River until they reached the vicinity of the old trading post, French Lick (present-day Nashville). This circuitous land route was necessary because the impenetrable Cumberland Plateau stood in the way of any direct travel from East to Middle Tennessee. Impressed by what they saw in the French Lick area, Robertson and his scouts returned to the Watauga region in late summer 1779, eager to launch the much-discussed removal.

The next few months were filled with busy preparations. By November the first group was ready to go; Robertson assembled about one hundred pioneers who said farewell to the land they had lived on for no more than nine years. They were to travel by horseback or on foot along the route Robertson had taken earlier in the year. Little is known about their trek to Middle Tennessee, except that they experienced an extremely cold winter and that they arrived on the banks of the Cumberland River, opposite French Lick, in late December. After resting a few days, Robertson and his fellow travelers walked across the frozen river on New Year's Day, 1780.

Meanwhile John Donelson had completed construction of his ark, appropriately named the "Adventure." He was now ready to assume command of the Cumberland armada, a flotilla of some two or three dozen boats that were to carry the second wave of pioneers to Middle Tennessee. Their water route was an incredible one: from Fort Patrick Henry (present-day Kingsport) down the Holston River to the Tennessee, then down it to the Ohio River, up the Ohio to the mouth of the Cumberland, and up the Cumberland River to the French Lick vicinity—approximately 1,000 miles. More than two hundred persons, a large percentage of whom were women and children, joined Donelson in this perilous voyage.

Infinitely more is known about this part of the Middle Tennessee migration because Donelson was mindful enough of posterity to keep a diary. While it does not provide all the details one might like, the journal nevertheless conveys enough of the drama of that frightful trip to cause most modern readers to confess gratitude for not having accompanied Donelson. A close reading might also lead to the sobering conclusion that the trip was in many respects a highly risky undertaking, perhaps excusable on the grounds that Robertson and Donelson really did not understand the potential dangers involved. They believed, for example, that the Wataugans' attack upon the Chickamauga towns on the Tennessee River in the spring of 1779 had remedied the problem of harassment by the Indians. Led by Dragging Canoe, the Chickamaugans were

---

Shown here is the first page of John Donelson's famous journal detailing his adventures during a 1,000-mile trip by water in 1780 from the Kingsport area to Nashville. Courtesy Tennessee Historical Society.

Journal of a Voyage, intended by Gods Permission, in the good Boat Adventure, from Fort Patrick Henry on Holston river, to the French Salt-Springs on Cumberland river, kept by John Donelson

---

Decemr. 22. 1779 — Took our Departure from the Fort and fell down the river to the mouth of Reedy Creek, where we were stopped by the fall of the water, and most excessive hard frost: and after much delay and many difficulties we arrived at the Mouth of Clouds Creek, on Sunday evening the 20th Febry. 1780 where we lay untill Sunday 27th. when we took our departure with sundry other vessels bound for the same voyage, and on the same day struck on the Poor-valey-Shoal, together with Mr Boyd and Mr Rounsifer, on which shoal we lay that afternoon & succeeding night in much distress.

Monday Febry 28th 1780 — In the morning, the water rising, we got off the shoal, after landing thirty persons to lighten our boat. In attempting to land on an island, received some damage and lost sundry articles, and came to Camp on the south shore, where we joined several other vessels also bound down.

Tuesday — Proceeded down the river & camped on the north shore [illegible]

dissident Cherokees who had established a few towns on the Tennessee River, some distance from the traditional Cherokee villages on the Little Tennessee River. After the devastation of the Chickamauga towns in the spring, these Indians merely moved farther down the river and built new settlements. Hence they were ready for Donelson's flotilla when it reached the vicinity of present-day Chattanooga in March of 1780.

The Donelson group left Fort Patrick Henry in late December 1779 (about the time of Robertson's arrival in Middle Tennessee) but did not reach its destination until four months later. Because of extremely bad weather and a drop in the river's level, the Donelson vessels moved an embarrassingly short distance of only three miles down the Holston River during the first two months of the voyage. Finally getting underway again in late February, Donelson's fleet had starvation, shipwreck, and attacks by unfriendly Indians yet ahead of it. The trip was swift and relatively uneventful until the water-borne pioneers reached the Chattanooga vicinity, where rapids in the river and Indian harassment provided excitement and danger. When they eventually approached the treacherous Muscle Shoals area of the Tennessee River, Donelson recorded their experiences in his journal:

> Here we did not know how soon we should be dashed to pieces, and all our troubles ended at once. Our boats frequently dragged on the bottom, and appeared constantly in danger of striking. They warped as much as in rough sea. But by the hand of Providence we are now preserved from this danger also.

From that adventure on to the completion of the journey, problems were relatively minor. Amazingly enough, all but about thirty of the original group survived the rigors of their water-borne invasion of Indian country and arrived at the Robertson settlement in late April 1780. Among those who successfully endured the arduous trip was Donelson's daughter, Rachel, later to become the wife of Andrew Jackson.

The approximately three hundred persons who made the Middle Tennessee migration probably thought that their troubles were over once they reached their destination, but serious difficulties lay ahead. For the moment, however, they desired to establish some kind of structured soci-

---

The minutes of the Cumberland committee bear eloquent testimony to the difficulties the pioneers experienced there in the early days of settlement. Courtesy Tennessee Historical Society.

North Carolina Cumberland River — Jan'y 7th 1783

The Manifold Sufferings & Distresses, that the Settlers here, have from Time to Time Undergone, Even Almost from our first Settling; With the Desertion of the Greater Number of the first Adventurers, Being so Discouraging to the Remaining Few; that All Administration of Justice Seemed to Cease from Amongst us; Which however Weak, Whether in Constitution, Administration, or Execution; Yet has been Construed in our favour; Against those Whose Malice, or Interest, Would Insinuate Us A People fled to A hiding place from Justice; And the Revival of them Again Earnestly Recommended: And now having a little Respite granted; And Numbers Returning to us; It Appears highly Necessary, That for the Common Weal of the Whole; The Securing of the Peace; The Performance of Contract Between Man & Man; Together with the Suppression of Vice Again to Revive our former Manner of Proceedings pursuant to the plan Agreed Upon at our first Settling here: And to Proceed Accordingly. Untill Such Times as it Shall Please the Legislature to grant us the Salutary Benefit of the law Duly Administered Amongst us by their Authority.

To this End previous Notice having been given to the Several Stations to Elect twelve Men of their Several Stations Whom they thought Most proper for the Business And being Elected to Meet At Nashborough the 7th day of Jan'y 1783 Accordingly there Met at the time And place Aforesd.

Col. Jas. Robertson | Heydon Wells
Capt. Geo. Freeland | Jas. Maulding
Thos. Molloy | Ebenezer Titus
Isaac Lindsey | Saml. Barton
David Rounsevall | Andrew Ewin

Constituting themselves into a committee for the purposes Aforesd. By Voluntarily Taking the following Oath Viz.

I, A. B., Do Solemnly Swear that as A Member of committee I will do Equal Right & Justice According to the best of My Skill And Judgment in all the Decision of All causes that Shall be laid before me Without Fear, Favour, or partiallity, — So help me God —

ety, and the outcome of this wish was the Cumberland Compact, authored by the ubiquitous and resourceful Richard Henderson. In May when the settlers affixed their signatures to this document, they agreed to create a rudimentary form of government, with twelve "judges" and an entry taker as the key posts of authority. They viewed this self-rule experiment as temporary, to last only until North Carolina could assert its control and law over the region. But the state did not do so until 1783, when it finally organized Davidson County. In the three-year interim, the Robertson-Donelson venture nearly failed, largely because of incessant Indian attacks which resulted not only in several deaths but also in a high departure rate of original settlers unwilling to face the terrifying risks any longer. With good reason some have said that only the steadfast courage and example of James Robertson in those dark days kept the new colony from completely surrendering to the threats and dangers of the wilderness. Despite "manifold suffering and distresses," as the January 1783 minutes of the Cumberland committee phrased it, the settlement endured. And when North Carolina set aside a goodly portion of Middle Tennessee as bounty land for Revolutionary War veterans, it assured the region's future.

While the Middle Tennessee settlement was being established, hundreds of miles away the conflicts in the southern theater of the American Revolution intensified. Those who lived in upper East Tennessee at the time were doubtless much more mindful of the Revolution than were the Middle Tennessee pioneers. As most native Tennesseans today know, their ancestors achieved military fame at the battle of King's Mountain. There in the northwestern section of South Carolina in October 1780, fighters from the Tennessee country, led principally by John Sevier, acquitted themselves astonishingly well against the British. It was a resounding victory for the patriot cause, and it assured Sevier of a lasting reputation as a public figure and leader.

Later in that same decade Sevier faced a quite different, but nonetheless difficult, challenge when he became the leader of the Franklin government. The so-called "Lost State of Franklin" came into being as a direct result of the actions of the North Carolina legislature. In an attempt to deal with the "problem" of the transmontane region, the General Assembly in June 1784 agreed to give its land beyond the mountains to the United States government, a decision that pleased land-hungry investors as well as those tidewater politicians who wanted to get rid of the bothersome Western problem. The action did not receive unqualified approval in North Carolina, however, and five months later, in November, the assembly bowed to the vocally hostile opposition by rescinding its earlier cession of the Western lands.

It was North Carolina's initial agreement to part with the transmontane region that stirred residents of upper East Tennessee to seek commitment among themselves for the formation of a state. Those who were so inclined first met in Jonesboro in August when they stipulated that they should meet later to establish a governmental structure. Accordingly, at a mid-December conclave provisional officers were elected, a provisional constitution was presented, and the name Franklin was adopted. A week or two after these actions were taken, John Sevier received word of North Carolina's decision to "re-annex" the Tennessee region.

But the news of North Carolina's latest resolution did not deter the leaders west of the mountains from their goal of forming a new state. Indeed, in the spring of 1785 the tempo of events quickened on both sides of the mountains. The embryonic Franklin government sent William Cocke to New York City, then the capital of the United States, to seek the Confederation Congress' approval of the admission of Franklin as the fourteenth state. This bold strategy did not succeed, however, because of the divided sentiment in Congress and because of the general weakness and ineptness of that body during this period. Meanwhile the Franklin and North Carolina governments unleashed manifestos and declarations against each other. With dire predictions of bloodshed and civil war, Governor Alexander Martin of North Carolina made a strong plea to the Franklinites: "That you be not insulted or led away with the pageantry of a mock government without the essentials—the shadow without the substance—which always dazzles weak minds . . . ." Franklin Governor John Sevier in reply castigated Martin's spineless attitude toward the Indians—a damaging charge in the eyes of Sevier's neighbors who shared his attitudes toward the Indians. Later in the year after the heated exchanges between the two governments had cooled a bit, the Franklin legislature met in Greeneville to consider a permanent constitution. Two competing documents were brought forward; the more democratic or radical one was rejected in favor of the one that was almost identical to the North Carolina constitution.

Despite the fast pace of the Franklin revolt, it appears that Sevier was a reluctant leader of the new state. Initially he had opposed the movement for separation from North Carolina, fearing that it might interfere with land speculating plans he had formulated with North Carolina associates, such as William Blount and Richard Caswell. These three men

A
DECLARATION OF RIGHTS

MADE BY

The REPRESENTATIVES of the Freemen of the State of FRANKLAND.

I. THAT all political power is vested in, derived from the people only.

II. That the people of this State ought to have the sole and exclusive right of regulating the internal government and police thereof.

III. That no man, or sett of men, are entitled to exclusive or separate emoluments or privileges from the community, but in consideration of public services.

IV. That the Legislative, Executive, and Supreme Judicial powers of government ought to be for ever separate and distinct from each other.

V. That all powers of suspending laws, or the execution of laws, by any authority, without the consent of the Representatives of the people, is injurious to their rights, and ought not to be exercised.

VI. That elections of members to serve as Representatives, in General Assembly, ought to be free.

VII. That, in all criminal prosecutions, every man has a right to be informed of the accusation against him, and to confront the accusers and witnesses with other testimony, and shall not be compelled to give evidence against himself.

had visions of a great land bonanza in the Muscle Shoals area of the Tennessee River, and they did not welcome any possible impediments to their plans. Moreover, when North Carolina organized the upper East Tennessee counties into a new military and judicial district in late 1784 and appointed Sevier as brigadier general of its militia, Sevier had additional reason to be less than enthusiastic about the Franklin cause. But Sevier shortly reversed himself, accepted election as Franklin's governor, and became the recognized leader of the western "revolt." Perhaps he changed his mind because he realized that the separation movement enjoyed widespread grass-roots support. And, perhaps he came to believe that a successful Franklin government could extend its boundaries southwest all the way to the great bend of the Tennessee River and thereby protect his hopes for land purchases there.

During his three years as governor, Sevier had to walk a narrow line between the pressures of his constituents and those of the rival government across the mountains. Usually he maintained a public posture of loud defiance toward North Carolina, and not unexpectedly he pursued an aggressive policy against the Cherokees. In fact, by 1786 he had pushed the Indian boundary line south to the banks of the Little Tennessee River, using both overt hostilities and treaty negotiations. Meanwhile, Sevier and North Carolina Governor Richard Caswell privately agreed upon a conciliatory policy to get North Carolina to accept peacefully the existence of the Franklin government by having Franklinites elected to the North Carolina legislature. In addition, however, Caswell shrewdly appointed officials in the Franklin counties to rival those already installed by the Franklin government, resulting in confusion and competing loyalties that played right into the governor's hands.

Other problems developed that spelled trouble for Sevier and the state of Franklin. For example, Sevier's chief nemesis was John Tipton, a Washington County neighbor, who became an arch-foe of the Franklin movement and fought against Sevier—even to the point of physical combat. Sevier also ran into trouble from an unexpected quarter: William Cocke, a strong proponent of the Franklin cause who, apparently jealous of Sevier, became increasingly antagonistic toward the Franklin

---

In the 1780s upper East Tennesseans created their own state, Franklin (spelled "Frankland" on this document). The declaration of rights served as the preamble to the Franklin constitution. Courtesy Tennessee Historical Society.

leader. Moreover, there is the lingering suspicion that some of the opposition within the state of Franklin grew out of an eagerness to participate in various land-speculating enterprises without Sevier's involvement or interference. Altogether these internal pressures eroded the solidarity and stability of the Franklin movement. Hopes for eventual success as a state were noticeably diminished when the framers of the new United States constitution in the summer of 1787 declared that "no new State shall be formed or erected within the Jurisdiction of any other State . . . without the Consent of the Legislatures of the States concerned as well as of the Congress" (Article IV, Section 3). It was highly unlikely that North Carolina would grant such consent.

A change in North Carolina governors hastened the doom of the Franklin government. Samuel Johnston, who evinced no love for Sevier or for most Westerners, immediately ordered the arrest of Sevier. Not surprisingly, it was John Tipton who eventually carried out Governor Johnston's decree and transported Sevier across the mountains to stand trial for high treason. Frontier justice being what it was, some of Sevier's friends rode into Morganton, helped Sevier escape from the courtroom, and whisked him back to Tennessee. Afterwards, North Carolina extended pardons to all who had participated in the Franklin movement, including John Sevier. By early 1789 North Carolina had effectively reasserted its control over the transmontane rebels and the state of Franklin was lost.

Middle Tennessee took no part in the Franklin experience of the 1780s. Instead, it was disturbed mainly by Indian atrocities that continued despite efforts at negotiating peace. Moreover, James Robertson and the Cumberland leaders engaged in a widely publicized intrigue with the Spanish government. The so-called conspiracy was rooted in two concerns: apprehensions about river navigation rights and a belief that the Spanish were stirring up the Indians against white settlers in the Tennessee country. Robertson even persuaded the North Carolina legislature in 1788 to name the Middle Tennessee district in honor of the Spanish governor of Louisiana, Don Estevan Miró. The area was thereafter known as the Mero District, spelled differently but nonetheless honoring the Spanish governor. John Sevier and other Franklin leaders also flirted with the Spanish authorities for a time, so that all of the Tennessee region talked about pledging allegiance to the Spanish king and separating from the United States. But it was really never much more than talk. The threat of Western secession was used to prod the North Carolina government into acceptance of the new United States constitution and the consequent surrender of its transmontane lands. The Spanish intrigue came to nothing when North Carolina finally ratified the national constitution and officially joined the Union in November 1789.

This long-awaited action by North Carolina set in motion the events that led to the creation of the federal territory out of its Western region. In December the area was ceded to the United States (much as had been done five years earlier) and in April 1790 the national government formally accepted it. This time, unlike in 1784, North Carolina did not change its mind and reappropriate its western lands, once it had transferred them; nor did residents of the Tennessee country attempt to form themselves into a new state. Perhaps the abortive Franklin experience had taught a lesson after all.

Congress then voted to establish the Southwest Territory, or more properly the Territory of the United States, South of the River Ohio—a misleading designation, inasmuch as the territory never included any area other than present-day Tennessee. Congress failed to enact a law to prescribe how the new territory was to be governed, merely stating that the Northwest Ordinance of 1787 would apply to the Southwest Territory (with the notable exception of the clause prohibiting slavery in the territory). Consequently, the next step was for Washington to appoint a territorial governor. The President shrewdly chose William Blount of North Carolina, a personal friend who also enjoyed strong support from the North Carolina congressional delegation. Blount was delighted with the appointment, particularly so because he had failed earlier to have the North Carolina legislature choose him for a United States Senate seat. Even more important, he believed the territorial gubernatorial post would enable him to profit financially from Western land speculations. As he wrote to a friend in June 1790, "my Western Lands had become so great an object to me that it had become absolutely necessary that I should go to the Western Country, to secure them and perhaps my Presence might have enhanced there [*sic*] Value. I am sure my present appointment will."

Despite his obvious enthusiasm, Blount did not arrive in the new territory until October 1790. He soon learned that he would have to deal with two major problems throughout his nearly six years as governor: administrative-political concerns and Indian affairs. To assist with the first of these, Blount wisely brought with him George Roulstone, a North Carolina printer and newspaper editor, who established the first newspaper in the territory. The paper afforded Blount a readily available means of presenting his views on key questions. Blount quickly as-

T H E

KNOXVILLE GAZETTE

[Vol. I.] SAT[illegible]RDAY, November 5, 1791. [No. 1.]

WE have now the pleasure of presenting the public with the FIRST NUMBER of the KNOXVILLE GAZETTE; and of making our acknowledgements to those gentlemen who so [illegible] forwarded our undertaking.

We will make it our study to merit a continuance of the favours we have received; and assure the public our utmost endeavours shall be exerted to make the Gazette worthy of their patronage.

We are the public's obedient humble servants,

G. ROULSTONE,
R. FERGUSON.

Printing-Office, Nov. 5, 1791.

TERMS of SUBSCRIPTION
FOR THE
KNOXVILLE GAZETTE.

The Gazette shall be published once in every two weeks.

Each subscriber to pay Two Dollars per annum, one half of which to be paid on subscribing, and the remainder in six months after.

RIGHTS of MAN:

Being an answer to Mr. Burke's attack on the FRENCH REVOLUTION,

BY THOMAS PAINE.

Secretary for foreign affairs to Congress in the American War, and author of a work entitled Common Sense.

AMONG the incivilities by which nations or individuals provoke and irritate each other, Mr. Burke's pamphlet on the French revolution is an extraordinary instance. Neither the people of France, nor the National Assembly, were troubling themselves about the affairs of England, or the English Parliament; and why Mr. Burke should commence an unprovoked attack upon them, both in parliament and in public, is a conduct that cannot be pardoned on the score of manners, nor justified on that of policy. [illegible]

[illegible] had neither spirit to undertake it, nor fortitude to support it; and now that there is none, he seeks an escape by condemning it.

Not sufficiently content with abusing the National Assembly, a great part of his work is taken up with abusing Dr. Price (one of the best hearted men that lives) and the two societies in England known by the name of the Revolution and Constitutional Societies.

Dr. Price had preached a sermon on the 4th of November, 1789, being the anniversary of what is called in England the Revolution, which took place in 1688. Mr. Burke, speaking of this sermon, says, 'The political divine proceeds dogmatically to assert, that by the principles of the revolution, the people of England have acquired three fundamental rights:

'1. To choose our own governors.

'2. To cashier them for misconduct.

'3. To frame a government for ourselves.'

Dr. Price does not say that the right to do these things exists in this or in that person, or in this or in that description of persons, but that it exists in the whole; that it is a right resident in the nation.—Mr. Burke, on the contrary, denies that such a right exists in the nation, either in whole or in part, or that it exists any where; and what is still more strange and marvellous, he says, 'that the people of England utterly disclaim such a right, and that they will resist the practical assertion of it with their lives and fortunes.' That men should take up arms, and spend their lives and fortunes, not to maintain their rights, but to maintain they have not rights, is an entire new species of discovery, and suited to the paradoxical genius of Mr. Burke.

The method which Mr. Burke takes to prove that the people of England have no such rights, and that such rights do not now exist in the nation, [illegible]

[illegible]

serted his authority over the counties in the territory, visiting them and constituting official governments for them. Recognizing that his erstwhile friend John Sevier was a potential troublemaker, Blount took steps to consummate a marriage of convenience between the two of them. Because of the provision that there should be a legislature once there were as many as 5,000 free adult males living in the territory, it was incumbent upon Blount to have a census taken. Although not finally completed until the summer of 1791, the census showed a total population of almost 36,000—which included nearly 6,300 free adult males, more than enough to entitle the territory to its own legislature. For the moment, however, Blount did not want to contend with a legislative body that might present additional headaches for his administration.

It was two years later, in 1793, before Blount eventually called for an election of a territorial legislature. He had apparently withstood all the pressures he cared to face alone as chief administrator and was now willing to share some of the responsibilities of government. The elections were held in December and the lower house met in Knoxville in February 1794. One of its chief duties was to draw up a list of names from which President Washington was to choose five men to serve as the upper house. Subsequently the two-house assembly convened in August; its second session was in June 1795.

By the latter date Blount had become a proponent of statehood, something he had heretofore opposed. A number of factors may have converted him to this new position: weariness of continuing as territorial governor, apprehensions about John Sevier's new restlessness, and aspirations to become a United States senator. He ordered a new census of the territory, and it revealed a total population of 77,200 of whom 66,600 were free persons—a figure which exceeded the requirement of 60,000 free inhabitants for statehood. A referendum for or against seeking statehood occurred simultaneously, and those favoring statehood won by a vote of 6,500 to 2,500. Accordingly, in November, Blount issued a call for an election of delegates to a constitutional convention that would meet in January 1796.

During his tenure as territorial governor, Blount had managed most

---

Making its appearance in November 1791, the Knoxville *Gazette* was Tennessee's first newspaper. The editor was George Roulstone, who accompanied William Blount from North Carolina to the Southwest Territory. Courtesy Tennessee Historical Society.

of the administrative-political problems adroitly. But matters of Indian affairs seemed to persist as a continuing threat—to governmental functions and to the lives of the white residents. Since Blount had been designated superintendent of Indian affairs by the act creating the territory, he was responsible under that title as well as being answerable as governor. He faced an Indian problem as soon as he took office. Because there were nearly 3,600 whites illegally residing south of the French Broad River, Blount had to deal immediately with the necessity of establishing new boundary lines with the Cherokees. The result was the Treaty of the Holston, signed in the summer of 1791, which pushed the Cherokee line just south of present-day Maryville.

Indians affairs were especially tormenting to Blount during the 1792–94 period. On the one hand, the settlers pleaded for governmental action to protect them from the Indians, who were accused of numerous atrocities. For example, the territorial legislature in the late summer of 1794 reported to Congress that Cherokees and Creeks had already killed 67 whites that year, in addition to wounding 10 and capturing 25 settlers, and had stolen 374 horses. But Secretary of War Henry Knox, on the other hand, repeatedly warned Blount not to take the offensive against the Indians. His anti-war policy grew out of the fact that Knox was bothered by an even more serious Indian menace in the Northwest. He simply wanted Blount to persevere until the Indians were brought under control elsewhere, which did not occur until General Anthony Wayne's victory at Fallen Timbers in August 1794. Knox's policy was violated, however, during Blount's absence from the territory in 1793, when John Sevier successfully chased and fought the Cherokees all the way into Georgia. But this offensive did not bring an end to the Indian threat, and the next year Blount yielded to the continual pressure for additional strikes against the Indians by condoning the successful "Nickajack Expedition," which was ordered by James Robertson against the Chickamaugans in the summer of 1794. It was well known throughout the territory in the early 1790s that the Spanish in the Louisiana and Florida areas had been partly responsible for stirring up the Indians in the western regions of the United States, hoping thereby to head off the advance of the Americans. But by 1795 a sudden calm prevailed, brought about in large measure by Robertson's successful attack and Wayne's victory in the Northwest, as well as by the new treaty with Spain in which the Spanish agreed to restrain the Indians in the West.

Despite the disruptions and threats represented by Indian problems, the population of the territory increased quite rapidly—from nearly

36,000 people in 1791 to more than double that number by the time of the 1795 census. Throughout the territorial period the population of East Tennessee was dominant, the area's eight counties accounting for almost 85 percent of the territory's residents in 1795. The difficulties associated with getting to the Middle Tennessee region obviously caused it to grow at a slower rate. As with the total population, the number of slaves more than doubled between 1791 and 1795, the 10,600 slaves in the latter year constituting about 14 percent of the territory's total population. Although East Tennessee had a larger number of slaves than did the Cumberland counties, the ratio of slaves to whites was higher in Middle Tennessee. Thus even at this early date the pattern was established whereby the slave population would be a more significant factor in the development of the middle part of the state than would be the case in the eastern counties.

Not only did East Tennessee dominate in terms of population, but it also held the upper hand in political and governmental matters. Participation in the Franklin movement of the 1780s perhaps gave the eastern section valuable experience in self-government that the middle counties lacked, since they were never a part of the Franklin experiment. Of greater direct importance, however, was Blount's decision to locate the territorial capital at the newly created town of Knoxville. Of necessity, then, the major political and governmental policies emanated from the eastern part of the territory. Even up to the time of the statehood referendum in the summer of 1795 the three Middle Tennessee counties opposed this new movement, apparently fearing even greater East Tennessee hegemony. Represented by only fifteen out of the fifty-five delegates, Middle Tennesseans understandably approached the constitutional convention with caution and skepticism.

Nevertheless, the requisite steps toward statehood were taken when delegates from the eleven counties assembled in Knoxville in early January 1796. Approximately one-third of the group was composed of men who either had already earned reputations as influential leaders or else were emerging as notables in politics and economics. The only important figure not a delegate to the convention was John Sevier, whose puzzling absence did not adversely affect his popularity. Within four weeks' time the convention completed its task of devising an instrument of government. Such rapidity may be attributed to several factors: heavy borrowing from the Pennsylvania and North Carolina constitutions, virtual unanimity on the kind of governmental structure desired, and some urgency to push Tennessee into the Union before the current session of

Congress adjourned. Without much debate or delay the delegates fashioned a constitution of moderate length, consisting of eleven articles.

The document itself contained few surprises; it was clearly a product of the times and region. Property and residency qualifications were prescribed for both voting rights and office holding. Free adult males, white and black, who met the specified qualifications were entitled to vote. Probably the most democratic feature of the constitution was the section regarding the election of militia officers: citizens subject to military duty were given the right to vote in these particular elections. This may explain in part why the county and state militias became important avenues of political advancement. The clause providing for the equal and uniform taxation of land (regardless of actual value) reflected the dominance of the land-holding wealthy interests at the constitutional convention. Incidentally, this provision continued to haunt the young government until it was changed by a new constitution in the 1830s. Given the overwhelming number of East Tennessee delegates, it is slightly surprising that the constitution stipulated that Knoxville would serve as the state capital only until the year 1802; afterwards, presumably any town might be chosen as the seat of government. The Mero delegates were insistent upon this arrangement and apparently the other framers went along with it in order to gain support for the entire document. Perhaps the most unexpected decision made at the convention was the delegates' vote to reduce their per diem allowance from $2.50 to $1.50—an action not duplicated by subsequent deliberative bodies in Tennessee's history.

Upon completion of the drafting of the constitution, the framers decided to speed a copy of it to Congress while that body was still in session. The action meant that Tennessee residents would not be given the opportunity to ratify or reject the new instrument of government. But the convention delegates apparently felt that getting Tennessee admitted to the Union in time to participate in the 1796 presidential election was more important than putting the constitution to a vote.

Very shortly after adjournment, a copy of the constitution was taken to Philadelphia, the nation's capital. But not until April did President Washington submit to Congress both the document and his recommendation in favor of statehood. Meanwhile, legislative and gubernatorial elections had been held in Tennessee in March. Quite predictably, Sevier

---

The governor's office is on the southside grounds of Blount Mansion. Courtesy of Bill Tracy Photography.

was chosen as governor, and the new legislature selected William Blount and William Cocke as the United States senators. But in Congress the question of admitting Tennessee became mired in obstructionism attributable to Jeffersonian control of the House and Federalist domination of the Senate. In the debates several Federalist congressmen raised objections to Tennessee statehood, most of which were red herrings to obscure the primary fear that Tennessee would become a pro-Jefferson state and would vote accordingly in the forthcoming presidential election. Eventually the opponents of statehood were worn down, some compromises reached, and on the next to last day of the session both houses agreed to accept Tennessee as the nation's sixteenth state. President Washington signed the bill on June 1, 1796, thereby creating the first state to emerge out of territorial status.

As one might expect, the leadership role of the infant state was quickly assumed by John Sevier, who served eleven years as governor (1796–1801 and 1803–1809). He excelled more as a symbolic figure for the state than as an efficient administrator, however, and in that sense might be called the George Washington of Tennessee. His immense personal popularity attracted support and devotion during the days of statehood, much as it had done since the 1770s. Yet despite his large following, Sevier had to contend with opposition. The most serious threat came from his cross-state rival, Andrew Jackson, whose personality and temperament closely paralleled Sevier's. Although their relationship had its ups and downs, Sevier and Jackson were generally antagonistic toward each other. Several incidents contributed to their hostility. In 1796, for example, Jackson lost the major generalship of the state militia to Sevier's candidate, George Conway; and six years later when Jackson and Sevier ran against each other for the state militia generalship, a tie vote resulted, which was broken in favor of Jackson by his friend, Governor Archibald Roane. Then, on a visit to Knoxville when Jackson encountered Sevier, a heated exchange of words followed in which Sevier declared that he knew of no service Jackson had rendered except to take a "trip to Natchez with another man's wife"—a painful reminder of the questionable circumstances surrounding Jackson's marriage to Rachel Donelson. Finally, in the 1803 gubernatorial campaign Jackson publicly disclosed unethical (some said scandalous) land deals made by Sevier years earlier, but Sevier was victorious nonetheless. These and other clashes between Jackson and Sevier led them to regard each other with something approaching outright contempt. This attitude, not surprisingly, made an impact upon statewide politics. A faction quickly coalesced around Sevier, for instance. Meanwhile, Jackson aligned himself with William Blount (whose expulsion from the United States Senate because of an alleged conspiracy with the British against Spanish Louisiana and Florida did not seem to bother his Tennessee constituents). Shortly, Jackson became one of the chief lieutenants of the Blount coterie. Such developments meant that state politics would be conducted on the basis of factions and personalities rather than political parties.

As had been true of William Blount, John Sevier and other governors during the state's formative period had to confront the question of Indian affairs. And, as time went on, Sevier and the later governors became increasingly embroiled in squabbles over public lands. These two concerns were inextricably linked because of the necessity of extinguishing Indian titles before *legal* settlement of a given area was possible. Ironically, the great Indian fighter, John Sevier, was virtually powerless as governor to do anything about the Indian "problem." Instead he, like his successors, had to look to the federal government. In the first year of statehood between two-thirds and three-fourths of the state was either occupied by Indians or claimed by them as hunting grounds. But beginning in 1798 and continuing through 1819, various treaties were negotiated with the Cherokees and Chickasaws. The most important of these occurred in 1818, when the Chickasaws surrendered their rights to the vast tract between the Tennessee and Mississippi rivers, and in 1819, when Secretary of War John C. Calhoun enticed the Cherokees to give up their lands between the Little Tennessee and Hiwassee rivers and retreat south of the Hiwassee. So successful were the various treaties that by 1820 the only Indians residing in the state were huddled in the southeastern corner. Doubtless the Indians sensed the futility of competing against an increasingly potent national government.

Tennessee's early years of statehood were marred by the continuing quarrels with North Carolina and the federal government over public lands. Congress intervened in 1806 to alleviate the chaotic situation by establishing a "Congressional Reservation," consisting of the southwestern corner of Middle Tennessee as well as the land between the Tennessee and Mississippi rivers, removing this area from possible settlement. At the same time Tennessee was authorized to handle the sticky matter of locating North Carolina land warrants elsewhere in the state. Many persons held warrants to lands in Tennessee either under terms of various North Carolina land laws of the 1780s or on the basis of military bounties to Revolutionary War veterans. For a time after passage of the congressional act, the interstate public lands controversy quieted. But in

1818, Congress, yielding to pressure from state officials, agreed to open up portions of the Congressional Reservation to satisfy the seemingly inexhaustible supply of North Carolina land warrants (many of which by this time were held by Tennesseans). Coupled with that decision was the successful "purchase" of West Tennessee from the Chickasaws. Thus parts of the western third of the state were to be opened to legal settlement. The army of land surveyors who marched into that region in 1819–20 were inhibited only by the presence of illegal squatters already scattered throughout the area. The town of Memphis, strategically located on the banks of the Mississippi River in the southwestern corner of the state, was hurriedly established once the western region was officially opened.

Although preoccupied by attempts to resolve the controversies over land, the state experienced a steady flourishing of economic activity. From the outset Tennessee was an overwhelmingly agricultural state. Corn, cotton, and tobacco quickly became chief crops, though East Tennessee cotton was never an important agricultural product. In the formative period the state exported agricultural commodities and imported manufactured goods; hence, trade and commerce received the attention even of those not directly involved in farming. Towns quickly became the centers of such activities, and the Cumberland and Tennessee rivers served as the very important natural avenues of exchange. The only manufacturing activity in this period, apart from the usual grist mills, looms, tanneries, and distilleries, was the fledgling iron industry which developed on a small scale in both East and Middle Tennessee. Even so, an 1810 report on Tennessee manufactures shows the liquor industry to have been a very productive and lucrative one, the total value in that year amounting to $401,000.

Despite the blossoming of the state's economy, there were no banks until the legislature chartered one in Nashville in 1807 and one in Knoxville in 1811. During the economic boom that followed the conclusion of the War of 1812, the legislature approved thirteen new banks. This sudden overexpansion of banking facilities mirrored the exaggerated optimism found especially in the Western states more than it reflected the economic well-being of the region. Shortly thereafter the inflated prosperity of both the nation and the state went into a tailspin. The precipitous drop in cotton prices gave the economic crisis a disturbing reality in Tennessee. In response to it, all of the banks in the state, except the Knoxville bank, immediately suspended the payment of specie, or hard money, to their customers.

Much like other Western states, Tennessee took steps to alleviate the depressed economy. In 1819, for example, the legislature passed a so-called "stay law," stipulating that no creditor could execute judgment against a debtor for two years—unless he was willing to accept depreciated paper money in payment of debts. Two years later the state's highest court struck down the "stay law" as unconstitutional, whereupon the legislature merely enacted another one. In 1820 the General Assembly established a state bank with authority to issue one million dollars of bank notes and to make small loans at 6 percent interest. The man behind these two major programs of relief and recovery was not the governor (Joseph McMinn) but rather Felix Grundy, a politician of established reputation both as congressman and as state legislator. It is debatable how significant these measures were in actually lifting the state out of the crisis, given the nationwide nature of the depression. But there seems to be little room for argument that these actions were important in a psychological sense—that is, in encouraging the belief that the state government was ready and able to extend a helping hand.

It is indicative of the severity of the crisis that independent-minded, self-sufficient Tennesseans should have looked to the government for solutions. For routinely the sturdy pioneer folk and the early citizens of the state turned to the comfort and strength of religion when weathering individual or group crises or when in need of simple inspiration. Among the possessions brought across the mountains, down the rivers and valleys was a God-fearing belief in some form of Protestant Christianity. The Scotch-Irish predominated among the earliest arrivals in the Tennessee wilderness, which almost by definition means that Presbyterianism prevailed. It left an indelible mark upon upper East Tennessee especially, for it is still quite noticeable today. Giants of the Presbyterian faith, such as Samuel Doak, Hezekiah Balch, and Samuel Carrick were instrumental in planting their beliefs deep in Tennessee soil. Within ten years of the beginning of permanent white settlements, Presbyterian churches were securely established, in the little towns as well as in the virtually inaccessible locations. Although thriving in East Tennessee from the outset, Presbyterian churches were not officially organized in Middle Tennessee until after the turn of the new century.

At about the time that Presbyterianism began to make headway in the middle part of the state, the "Great Revival" in Kentucky and Tennessee erupted. Thousands attended camp meetings and equally large numbers, caught up in the enthusiastic revival preaching, found religion. The denominations that benefited most directly and to the greatest extent from the frontier revival movement were the Baptist and Methodist. Traditional Presbyterianism, with its emphasis upon Calvinist tenets and an educated clergy, could not compete successfully for converts in the heat of the rejection of Calvinism and a learned ministry. Generally speaking, the Presbyterians lost out numerically from this point on. A group of Presbyterians in Middle Tennessee, however, under the influence of the preaching of William McGee, seceded from main-line Presbyterianism in 1810 to establish the Cumberland Presbyterian Church—the only religious group owing its origins solely to Tennessee. Some Presbyterians eventually followed the leadership of Barton Stone and Alexander Campbell to embrace a new movement to unite all of the Protestant denominations and to restore the New Testament church. The Campbellite cause began to make significant headway after 1820, when it began attracting Baptists to its banner. In time Tennessee would become one of the strongest Campbellite regions in the entire nation.

While the free-flowing waters of revivalism were sweeping across the state, there were conscientious Tennesseans who directed their concern to matters of the mind. Quite often the same people who promoted organized religion were also advocates of formal education—the best example being the Presbyterians. Permanent white settlers had hardly been in upper East Tennessee a full ten years when the Reverend Samuel Doak established Martin Academy and the Salem Presbyterian church; both are still in existence today in the Jonesboro vicinity. In the 1790s Martin Academy's name was changed to Washington College, to honor the nation's first president. In Middle Tennessee the Reverend Thomas Craighead, also a Presbyterian divine, organized Davidson Academy, chartered in 1785. It subsequently became Cumberland College (1806) and then the University of Nashville (1826). Reflecting the strong interest in formal learning at the higher levels, the first plenary session of the territorial legislature chartered two colleges in 1794, Greeneville and Blount, with the Reverend Hezekiah Balch as the head of the former and the Reverend Samuel Carrick as the leader of the latter. Both men, it should be recalled, were Presbyterian ministers. Greeneville College

---

(*Above*): Established first as Martin Academy by the Reverend Samuel Doak, this school's name was changed to Washington College. Courtesy Tennessee Historical Society. (*Below*): Among the earliest maps of Tennessee was this one published in *Carey's American Pocket Atlas.* Courtesy American Antiquarian Society.

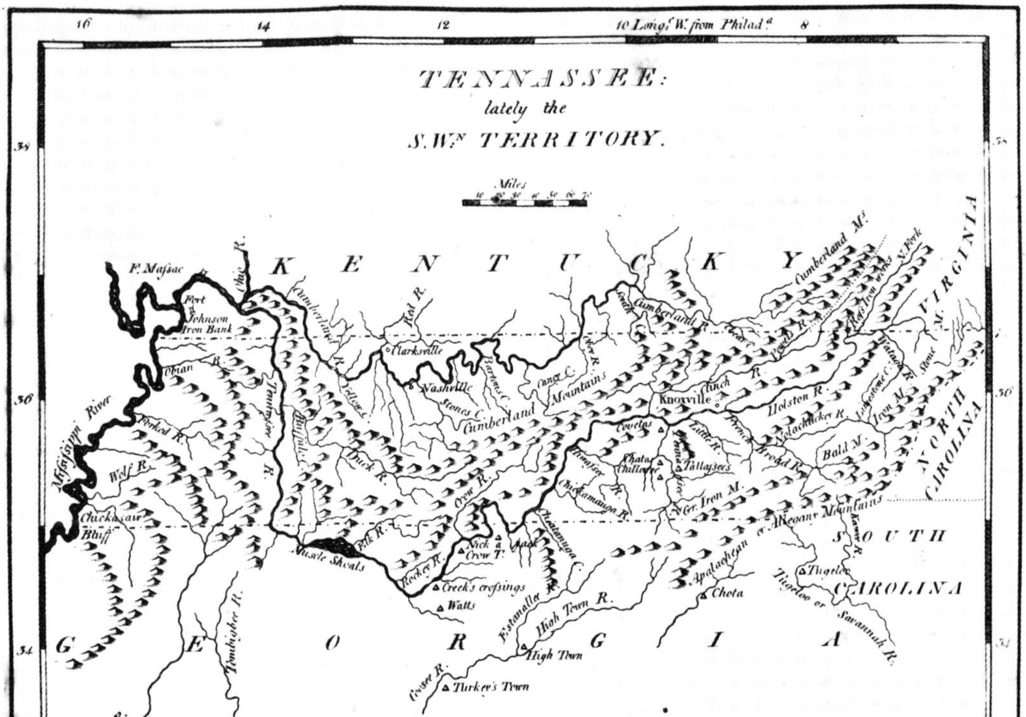

W. Barker sculp.

remained in existence until after the Civil War when it merged with Tusculum College in the same town. Blount College evolved into East Tennessee College, then East Tennessee University, and finally (in the 1870s) into the University of Tennessee.

Despite the impressive progress made during Tennessee's formative period in behalf of education, little was done to provide for pre-college schooling—a situation common to the Southern states. There was nothing even resembling a public school system, though there was a handful of private academies scattered around the state. Quite frequently, an individual and his neighbors would get together to build a one-room schoolhouse in hopes of attracting a teacher to come and provide instruction for the children of the area. A classic example of this occurred in Blount County in the mid-1790s when Andrew Kennedy and his neighbors constructed a log schoolhouse near Maryville. Strong historical tradition holds that in about 1811 or 1812 an energetic, adventuresome teenager, Sam Houston, took on the responsibilities of schoolmaster of the Kennedy school. Although his tenure there was very brief, the experience of teaching in this simple schoolhouse made a lasting impression upon Houston. The building has fortunately been preserved and is still standing today—representative of the only kind of education available to most Tennesseans in the days before public schools.

While there might be some debate about the significance of schools and churches in the development of early Tennessee, no one would argue the importance of an ever-expanding population upon the evolution from frontier to statehood. In fact, during the 1790–1830 period Tennessee's rate of population growth exceeded that of the nation's. By the time the first federal census was taken in Tennessee (1800), the number of inhabitants had increased threefold over the population figures shown in the 1791 territorial census. In 1810, Middle Tennessee moved ahead of the eastern section in population for the first time. And in the following decade, East Tennessee's total number of inhabitants increased only 34,000 while Middle Tennessee's swelled by over 125,000—thereby assuring the latter section of continued dominance in population. West Tennessee had been officially open for only one year when the federal census of 1820 showed that slightly fewer than 2,000 persons were residing there. Statewide there were 423,000 Tennesseans at the time of the census. Unquestionably then, by this date Tennessee's sometimes awkward, sometimes difficult, formative years were over. With nearly a half million inhabitants the state stood ready to embark upon a new period of progress and prominence.

2. The Maturing Years, 1820–1860

Tennessee matured in the four decades before the Civil War and in the process captured a moment or two in the national spotlight, mainly because of politics. Two Tennesseans won the presidency and several others achieved prominence; it was a sort of political golden age. But politics was not the sole consuming concern of the period, for great strides were also made in economic development. Tennessee played a vital role in Southern agriculture and in the interregional flow of goods and products. Slavery, while not exclusively an economic institution, was an integral part of the material progress and well-being of the state, although the slave system created many distresses at the same time—especially for the black population and perhaps for some whites.

These were not only maturing but also busy years. In the 1820s, for example, West Tennessee served as the new frontier, when incredible numbers of people—approximately 140,000—swarmed into that region virtually overnight. Equally exhilarating was the launching of Andrew Jackson's national political career that culminated in his election as President in 1828. Meanwhile closer to home, William Carroll for six terms graced the governor's chair with the rare quality of effective leadership. Various developments in the 1830s sustained the accelerated pace of the state's life: two-party politics emerged for the first time; scores of Tennesseans, not the least of whom was David Crockett, headed for Texas to fight for its independence; some even went to Florida to fight Seminole Indians; a new state constitution drafted in 1834 brought more democracy; and certain reforms of penal and mental institutions, long urged by Governor Carroll, were initiated. Andrew Jackson lived long enough to derive immense pleasure from the 1845 presidential inauguration of his protégé and fellow Tennessean, James K. Polk. A year later thousands of Tennesseans answered President Polk's call to participate in the Mexican War. In the 1850s the railroad mania hit Tennessee with full steam, great accomplishments crowning the arduous efforts of fi-

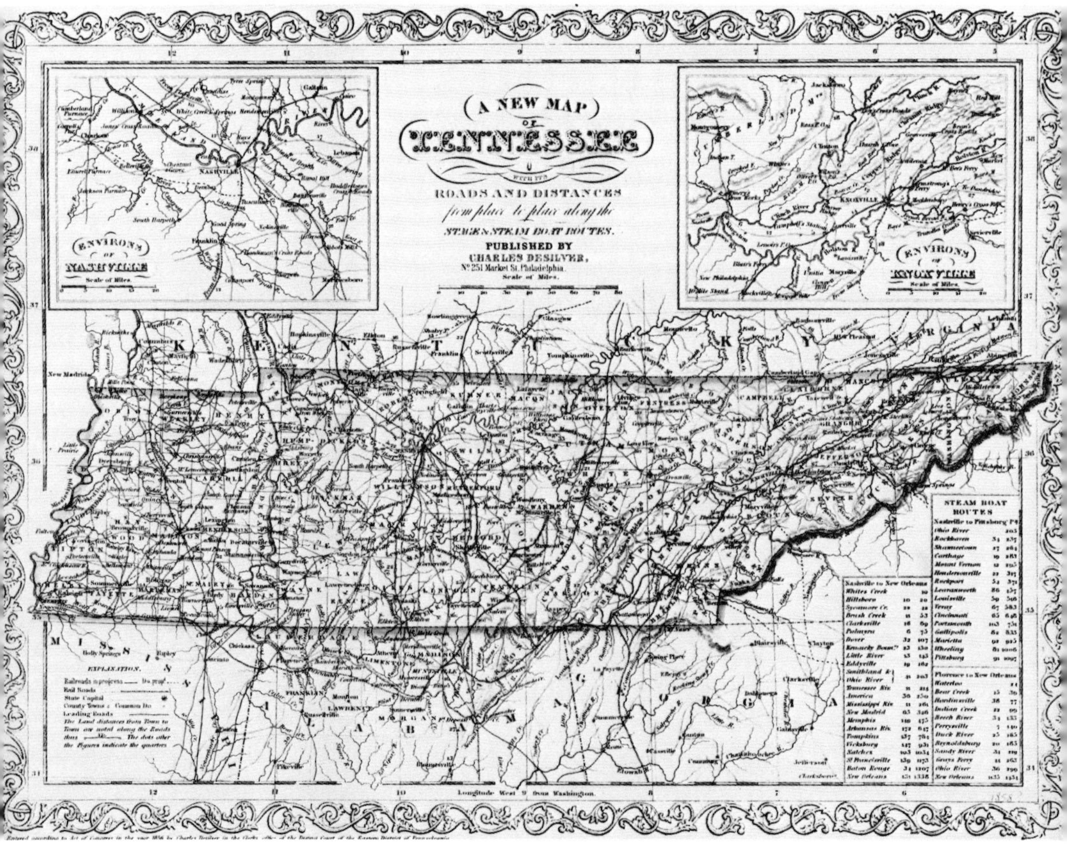
A NEW MAP
OF
TENNESSEE
WITH ITS
ROADS AND DISTANCES
from place to place along the
STAGE & STEAM BOAT ROUTES.
PUBLISHED BY
CHARLES DESILVER,
No. 251 Market St. Philadelphia.
Scale of Miles.
ENVIRONS OF NASHVILLE
ENVIRONS OF KNOXVILLE
STEAM BOAT ROUTES
EXPLANATION.
Longitude West 9 from Washington.

nanciers and common laborers alike. And finally, the ominous cloud of the North-South sectional dispute began to impress many Tennesseans with the uncertainty of the preservation of the Union.

Tennessee was to lose its status as a frontier state during these years preceding the Civil War as land-hungry homesteaders and other adventuresome spirits pushed onward to newer frontiers to the south, southwest, and midwest. Thus the decade of the 1820s was the last period of rapid population growth for Tennessee. During those ten years the state added more than a quarter of a million residents, swelling the total population to about 682,000 in 1830. And twenty years later, even though population growth had slowed and the state was losing more people through out-migration than it was gaining through in-migration, Tennessee reached the milestone of one million inhabitants. Within its Grand Divisions, East Tennessee had already lost ground, relatively speaking, to Middle Tennessee, which in 1820 boasted nearly 68 percent of the state's total population. Next it was West Tennessee's turn to expand, a growth that precipitously dropped Middle Tennessee's share of the population to only slightly more than 50 percent in 1830 and to 46 percent in 1860. In 1850, the population of West Tennessee, its agricultural prosperity attracting thousands of new residents, almost matched that of East Tennessee, and ten years later the eastern and western thirds of the state had identical numbers of residents (the two sections combined accounting for about 598,000 of the 1,110,000 state total). The number of people living in towns and cities was still small—only about 4.2 percent of Tennessee's population. But the year 1860 saw Memphis, which was hardly more than a geographical expression in 1820, emerge as the state's largest city. Its population increased two and a half times during the 1850s to reach 22,600. Nashville, formerly the most heavily populated city, dropped to second place with a total of 17,000 inhabitants, while Knoxville reported only 3,700 residents.

What were the main interests of this predominantly rural population, aside from its home and church life and the necessity of making a living? Some observers have pointed to politics, which was said to have been a consuming passion for scores of Tennesseans while serving also as a

---

(*Above*): Late in the antebellum period, the state capitol in Nashville occupied a prominent spot in the city's skyline. From *Harper's Weekly*, March 8, 1862. (*Below*): This map reflects Tennessee in the late 1850s. Courtesy Special Collections, University of Tennessee Library.

kind of social outlet. Although at no time during this 1820–60 era was more than 17 percent of the Tennessee population eligible to vote, the impact of politics reached far beyond this circumscribed number. Literally thousands of these rural residents were attracted to the nearby towns and villages for the colorful, informative, and socially-oriented rallies and political contests. Contributing to politics' widespread and irresistible spell were such factors as the energetic and skillful political leadership that was present, and the fierce competitiveness of the two-party system. The rallies and barbecues exerted a strong mass appeal, somewhat like that of the religious camp meetings of an earlier day. In addition, the development of a vigorous partisan newspaper network helped sustain interest and inflame political feelings. The record shows that some kind of statewide campaign and election took place in thirty of the forty years of this period.

State politics in the 1820s assumed new dimensions of interest primarily because of the evolution of Jackson as a presidential contender. To promote Jackson's cause, John Overton, William B. Lewis, and John H. Eaton successfully took over leadership of the old Blount faction and subsequently pressured the legislature to elect Jackson to the United States Senate in 1823. Their machinations met some resistance, however, from a new political group headed by Andrew Erwin; it arose from the ashes of the old Sevier coalition which had disintegrated after Sevier's death in 1815. The most promising star of the Erwin group was the governor, William Carroll, whose elevation as a leader of "democratic" policies was opposed, oddly enough, by his erstwhile friend Andrew Jackson. But after Jackson's election to the presidency, the pro-Jackson faction found itself divided. Some Jackson leaders in Tennessee resented the newly exalted status of Overton, Lewis, and Eaton and broke away to form a second Jacksonian clique. Felix Grundy and James K. Polk were two of the principal figures in this "young Turks" group. The two pro-Jackson factions were spared an internal battle, potentially bruising, when Governor Sam Houston, the Jacksonian incumbent, suddenly resigned his office in 1829, left his bride of only three months, and went west under a cloud of mystery. Before this turn of

---

Andrew Jackson, one of two Tennesseans serving as President in the antebellum period, was a forceful and controversial leader of the nation. This print appeared after he left the presidency. Courtesy Special Collections, University of Tennessee Library.

HERMITAGE
Andrew Jackson

events, the Grundy-Polk group had been threatening to back the Erwin gubernatorial candidate, Carroll, instead of Houston.

In the 1830s, Tennessee politics was highlighted by the revolt against Jackson and the consequent evolution of the two-party system. The spark that ignited the anti-Jackson conflagration in Tennessee was the President's decision to make Martin Van Buren of New York his heir apparent and successor. In the 1835 governor's race, Newton Cannon, capitalizing on the antipathy toward Van Buren, launched the revolt by scoring a victory. Shortly thereafter came Hugh Lawson White's bid for the presidency in 1836. Being a native Tennessean, White's candidacy naturally evoked state pride—much as Jackson's own campaigns had done. Although breaking with Jackson and running against Van Buren, White insisted that he was the only true Jacksonian in the race. President Jackson rushed into the state to take direct command of the effort to put down rebellion among the home folk, but to no avail. No sooner had White carried Tennessee than the gubernatorial campaign of 1837 commenced, and the incumbent, Cannon, taking advantage of the vulnerability of his Jackson-allied opponent, won a stunning victory. By this time politics at the national level had developed to the point of having two distinct parties. Those swept along by Jackson's triumphs were known as Democrats, the direct descendants of the old Jeffersonian party. Opposition to President Jackson gave rise to a party called the Whigs, a label indicative of a belief in the supremacy of the legislative branch over the executive. Under the tutelage of men such as Henry Clay, Whigs at the national level advocated governmental involvement in the nation's economy. For the moment, however, a clearcut two-party arrangement did not yet exist in Tennessee in any official sense. But by the 1839 gubernatorial race, there was no question that Cannon sought re-election as a Whig, while Polk worked for victory as a devout Jacksonian Democrat. These two contenders established a new tradition in Tennessee politics when they staged joint appearances and debates throughout the state. Proving himself the master of this new style of rough and tumble politics, Polk snatched victory away from Cannon. Polk's surprising win in 1839 helped stem the tide of Whiggery and "redeem" the state, however momentarily, from its desertion of the Jacksonian cause.

Two-party competition became entrenched very quickly. The hard-cider and log-cabin ballyhoo offered by the Whigs in behalf of "Tippecanoe and Tyler too" in the presidential campaign of 1840 successfully ushered in the period. In the 1841 and 1843 gubernatorial contests, Tennessee Whigs caught the Democrats off guard by running an obscure but colorful opponent, James C. ("Lean Jimmy") Jones, against Polk. Both times Jones defeated the exasperated Polk, who was seldom able to match Jones's talent for anecdotes and yarns. To compound Polk's misfortunes, he failed to carry his own state in the 1844 presidential battle—losing to Henry Clay by a scant three hundred votes. The string of statewide Whig victories was not broken until Polk's close political ally, Aaron V. Brown, defeated the Whigs in the 1845 governor's race. Looking at the decade, one sees that the Whigs won all three presidential elections and three of the five gubernatorial contests. The races were breathtakingly close, however. No victorious governor, for example, received as much as 52 percent of the statewide vote. Furthermore, elections during this decade were characterized by incredibly high percentages of voter turnout, thanks both to the excitement generated by the candidates and the intense two-party rivalry. Generally, Middle Tennessee, Jackson's home section, voted Democratic, whereas East and West Tennessee, centers of anti-Jackson sentiment, boosted the fortunes of the Whig party.

The ten years leading up to the Civil War were marked by shifting political alignments, emergence of new parties, and, significantly, the demise of the Whig party at both the national and state levels. The Whigs, in fact, failed even to field a candidate for state office in Tennessee after the 1853 governor's race. Despite the absence of a formal Whig party, however, resistance to the Jacksonians did not end in Tennessee, for the Know Nothing and then the Opposition parties quickly emerged as safe havens for old-line Whigs. Two-party rivalry thus continued throughout the decade, although not with the same parties that had been fighting each other since the late 1830s. Amid such political disarray and confusion, the Democrats managed to win all the statewide elections from 1853 to the end of the decade. The lack of two strong, well-defined parties undoubtedly contributed to the decline in levels of voter turnout and to widening gaps between the vote totals of victorious and defeated candidates. Another political shift of the period was that West Tennessee had gravitated into the Democratic camp by the mid-1850s, leaving only East Tennessee as the stronghold of the anti-Jacksonian cause.

Tennesseans meanwhile were finding that their first governing document, signed in 1796, needed to be rewritten to meet the needs of a growing, developing state. Paramount among the problems demanding a solution was the bothersome question of taxation. Economic and demographic changes that had taken place since 1796 had rendered the clause

providing for the equal and uniform taxation of property increasingly antiquated and unfair. A chaotic and inefficient judicial system, long criticized by knowledgeable individuals, was also in desperate need of reform. For some, this goal of judicial change in itself justified the writing of a new constitution. Consequently, although calls for a constitutional convention were rejected by the voters in 1819 and again in 1831, the requisite number of favorable votes was finally obtained in 1833, setting in motion the election of convention delegates. When the delegates were chosen in March 1834 for their spring meeting that year, the action was accompanied by the warning of one observer: " . . . if we cannot get more talents in the Convention than we have in the Legislature I tremble for our Constitution."

There were sixty delegates who met in Nashville in mid-May to devise a new and acceptable instrument of government. They did not finish until the end of August. Two-thirds of the delegates were farmers, with most of the remainder being lawyers. A majority of the delegates were inexperienced in terms of public or government service, but they drew up a constitution that was subsequently approved by the people and that served the state for the next thirty-five years.

The key provisions of their handiwork were in keeping with expectations. The hotly debated taxation question, for example, was resolved in favor of the revisionists who wanted property taxed according to its value. The only opposition to this came from the delegates representing prosperous Middle Tennessee. The state judicial system was revamped with a clearly defined supreme court at the head of this branch of government. Bowing to intrastate sectionalism, the framers decreed that the new court should be composed of three judges, one from each division of the state. Property qualifications for both voting and officeholding were dropped; all county offices were made elective rather than appointive. On the question of the permanent location of the state capital, the delegates hedged by declaring that the legislature in 1843 must make the final decision. Petitions from sixteen counties urging some form of emancipation of slaves forced the constitution framers to confront this controversial problem, despite the desires of some delegates, and the issue consumed a good bit of the convention's time. By a close vote the

---

In this print, James K. Polk clearly shows the strain of his presidential office; he lived only three months after his term expired in 1849. Courtesy Special Collections, University of Tennessee Library.

convention eventually adopted a clause that prohibited the legislature from acting favorably on emancipation. Closely akin to this controversy was the matter of voting rights. After enlarging the franchise by eliminating property qualifications, the convention agreed that free black adult males should no longer enjoy the right to vote in Tennessee. Paradoxically, then, the new constitution which contained democratizing provisions also stripped from one group of citizens the fundamental right of democracy —the right to vote. Democracy's banquet table was not spread for all.

Having completed their work, the delegates stipulated that there should be a statewide vote on the constitution, but only those individuals who qualified to vote under the provisions of the new constitution would be eligible to participate in the referendum. The ratification vote was held in March 1835, at which time 71.4 percent of the voters favored the new document. Altogether fifty-eight out of the sixty-two counties ratified it, the four nonconforming counties being located in Middle Tennessee. Across the state the people expressed their approval in a resounding way and the new constitution went into effect immediately.

That the constitutional convention wrestled with questions regarding slavery and free blacks is not surprising, given the impact that blacks made upon antebellum society. Slavery in Tennessee did not differ appreciably from slavery in other Southern states, for it was essentially a socioeconomic institution tied to agricultural activity and productivity. The following table provides a convenient summary of some pertinent facts about the size and distribution of the slave population. It can be seen that the slave population increased at a faster rate than the rest of the population, the proportion of the state's inhabitants who were slaves standing at 22.1 percent in 1840 but rising to 24.8 percent in 1860. It is also apparent from these figures that East Tennessee had relatively little involvement with slavery, whereas Middle and West Tennessee were very dependent upon bondsmen. When one considers the total population of the three sections, it is significant that one-third of West Tennessee's inhabitants (in 1860) were slaves—a fact indicative of that section's massive cotton growing activity.

Despite the size of the slave population, the number of slaveholders was quite small. In 1860, for example, the white population of the state was approximately 827,000, but the total number of slaveowners was only 36,844 (or about 4½ percent). Furthermore, less than 3,000 Tennessee slaveholders owned more than twenty slaves. By sections, there were about 4,800 slaveowners in East Tennessee, 18,500 in Middle, and 13,500 in West Tennessee.

Slave trading flourished in the state despite an 1826 law designed to stop the importation of slaves for purposes of resale. Tennessee's geographical location, between the older slave areas of the South and the

SLAVE POPULATION STATISTICS

	number of slaves (1840)	*number of slaves* (1860)	*percent of state's slave population* (1840)	*percent of state's slave population* (1860)	*percent of population that was slave* (1840)	*percent of population that was slave* (1860)
East	19,915	27,500	11.0	10.0	8.8	9.0
Middle	106,640	148,000	58.0	54.0	26.0	29.0
West	56,500	100,200	31.0	36.0	29.2	33.5
State	183,000	275,700	—	—	22.1	24.8

newer, expanding slave regions of the Southwest, made the state a natural avenue for the slave traffic. Nashville and especially Memphis became recognized centers of the slave trade. Perhaps in exasperation, the legislature in 1855 rescinded the 1826 law and gave official sanction to the traffic in slaves that had been thriving for years. Slave traders and slaveowners were encouraged by the substantial rise in the average monetary value of a Tennessee slave in the 1850s from $547 to $855. The vast majority of these slaves were engaged in agriculture—cotton, tobacco, and grains—but some labored in the few scattered industries, some were skilled craftsmen, and an appreciable number were domestic servants. Little is known about the non-farm slaves, although both Memphis and Nashville had slave populations in excess of 3,000 by 1860.

In contrast to the commonly held notion that slaves were controlled solely by their masters, a slave in antebellum Tennessee was entitled to trial by jury, to the usual procedures of grand jury indictment, and to legal counsel—furnished by the state if the slave's master refused to provide an attorney. Tennessee slaves seeking legal remedy for promised manumission frequently found the state's courts friendly to their claims. The record also shows that slaves victimized by procedural wrongs in lower courts had hopes of relief from the state supreme court. In the 1850s, for instance, a slave who was an accused rapist had his conviction overturned by the state's highest court which chastised the lower court for both jury misconduct and the omission of material portions of evidence. The supreme court heard the case again three years later and acquitted the slave because he had not been given a trial by an impartial jury. In an 1839 case the state supreme court rendered an eloquent pronouncement in behalf of the status of slaves in the judicial process: "the law . . . takes the slave out of the hands of his master, . . . treats the slave as a rational and intelligent human being, responsible to moral, social, and municipal duties and obligations, and gives him the benefit of all the forms of trial which jealousy of power and love of liberty have induced the freeman to throw around himself for his own protection." One of the most intriguing litigations occurred in the 1840s when Loyd Ford of Washington County stipulated that upon his death his slaves should be freed and be given Ford's 112-acre farm—this despite the fact that Ford had seven sons. Not unexpectedly, Ford's children in due time contested the provisions of the will. After several different court proceedings, however, the state supreme court eventually ruled in favor of freedom for Ford's slaves and also gave them the property.

Most of the relatively few slaves in Tennessee who acquired freedom did so by virtue of private manumission, for organized efforts to promote statewide emancipation were singularly ineffective. With the exception of a small antislavery group in Middle Tennessee that existed for only twelve months, all of the organized antislavery activity was confined to East Tennessee—the region least dependent upon slavery. In 1819 Elihu Embree began the publication of an antislavery newspaper in Jonesboro, *The Manumission Intelligencer,* reputed to be the first such newspaper in the nation, and in 1822 Benjamin Lundy arrived in Greeneville to publish his antislavery paper, *The Genius of Universal Emancipation.* But Embree's death after only a few issues of his paper were published and Lundy's departure after less than three years of publishing left the state without any antislavery publications. For a time, Methodists, Presbyterians, and Quakers—again, mainly in East Tennessee—worked in support of gradual emancipation. Yet despite such apparent signs of vitality, the movement was short-lived and without widespread following. In the 1830s as the national antislavery movement grew and intensified, the Tennessee effort evaporated, largely because defenders of slavery became more active and vocal in the face of the growing menace of abolitionism. The last Tennessee voice to be heard was that of Ezekiel Birdseye, a Newport resident who urgently desired the emancipation of slaves. In the early 1840s he tried to promote a scheme whereby East Tennessee would sever its ties with the state and form a separate free state. This somewhat quixotic proposal died quickly, but not before eliciting some support in East Tennessee. After all, in the opinion of several of that section's leaders, one of the evils of slavery was that it had enabled Middle and West Tennessee to thrive and prosper.

The few free blacks who lived in Tennessee—they never totaled as much as 1 percent of the state's population—were either former slaves who had gained their freedom or were blacks who had never been slaves. Despite their small numbers (7,300 in 1860), they caused apprehensions in the white-dominated society which made several efforts to control the blacks' activities. Free blacks were required to register and carry registration papers with them at all times, for instance, and the 1831 legislature prohibited free blacks of other states from moving into Tennessee. The same legislature went even further, requiring any Tennessee slave being freed to leave the state, but this particular ban was later lifted.

Although their activities and rights were circumscribed by state law, free blacks nevertheless managed to occupy the twilight zone of freedom fairly successfully. Civil rights were virtually nonexistent, but property rights were relatively unrestricted for them. A free black could make a contract, inherit and own property, buy and sell, sue and be sued. Nearly all free blacks engaged in menial and manual labor, but some prospered in more skilled jobs. Sherod Bryant of Davidson County, the wealthiest free black in the state in 1850, was a successful farmer who owned twenty-two slaves. According to the 1860 census reports on 5,874 free blacks in thirty-nine counties, they held real and personal property valued at nearly $713,000. But whatever material successes might have been enjoyed by some, all free blacks daily felt the burden of their anomalous position in society. Especially was this true in matters of social relations, for free blacks could not associate with whites and could socialize with slaves only by permission. It was at best a difficult and degrading station in life, analogous to being a prison inmate out on parole.

As previously indicated, most of Tennessee's antebellum blacks, slave and free, were tillers of the soil and consequently were important to the state's agricultural economy. Not only were Middle and West Tennessee the sections with the largest number of slaves, but they also were the chief centers of agricultural productivity. Cotton was the main cash crop in Tennessee, although about 80 percent of it was grown in a cluster of only five counties in the southwestern corner of the state. The remainder was produced in the central part of Middle Tennessee. Tobacco, which was second to cotton in cash income, was also confined largely to Middle and West Tennessee. Some tobacco was raised in the eastern third of the state, but production there was no match for the volume raised in the other two sections. As the table below shows, with the exception of corn alone, the state produced much more in 1860 than it had in 1850. The dramatic increase in wheat production in the 1850s was brought about, to a large extent, by East Tennessee's commitment to grow wheat for export purposes; in fact, it led the state in the production of wheat. Even though the state experienced notable expansion of agricultural productivity in this decade, national rankings improved only for tobacco. The tremendous boom in farming activities in the Midwest and the Southwest in the 1850s accounts for Tennessee's slippage in national measurements.

AGRICULTURAL PRODUCTIVITY

	1850	*national rank*	*1860*	*national rank*
Cotton (bales)	194,500	5th	296,400	8th
Corn (bushels)	52,276,000	5th	52,090,000	6th
Tobacco (pounds)	20,149,000	4th	43,448,000	3rd
Wheat (bushels)	1,619,000	13th	5,459,000	13th
Value of livestock	$29,978,000	4th	$50,211,000	7th
Cash value of farms	$97,851,000		$271,359,000	

Tennessee broke away from conventional crop production by turning to the cultivation and manufacture of silk in the two decades prior to the Civil War. The simplicity and low cost of raising silkworms appealed especially to small farmers in the state, just as it did throughout the nation; the farmers thus busily planted mulberry trees for the silkworms to feast upon. The 1840s was the great period of silk in Tennessee. The legislature offered a bounty of ten cents a pound on cocoons and fifty cents a pound on reeled silk. Governor James C. Jones appeared at his 1843 inauguration wearing a suit of Tennessee manufactured silk. And by 1850 the state led the entire nation in the production of cocoons (nearly 2,000 pounds). Within the state's three sections, East Tennessee produced the greatest quantity of silk. But shortly after Tennessee's record-breaking silk crop occurred, tremendous numbers of silkworms began dying off, so that by 1860 the state produced only seventy-one pounds of cocoons. The great dream of an empire of silk in Tennessee and the South vanished about as quickly as it had first appeared.

Among numerous agricultural journals published in the state was *The Tennessee Farmer.* This May 1835 issue took up silk cultivation. Courtesy Special Collections, University of Tennessee Library.

THE TENNESSEE FARMER.

No. 6.] JONESBOROUGH, MAY 1835. [Vol. 1.

BY THOMAS EMMERSON, AT $1 PER ANNUM IN ADVANCE—OR $1 50 AT THE END OF THE YEAR

THE SILK CULTURE.

The importance of the subject to which it relates, the time required for making the necessary preparations, in rearing the mulberry, building the houses, and acquiring dexterity in all the various operations connected with the manufacture—the demonstrations of the practicability of success afforded by the actual experiments which have been made in Connecticut and other parts of the United States—and the vast benefits which would result to Tennessee from the extensive and successful culture of silk, will, we trust, be deemed a sufficient apology for occupying so large a portion of the present number with the subjoined article from that valuable paper the American Farmer and Gardener.

It will be seen by the letter of Judge Spencer of New York, one of the most talented men in the nation, that the subject has attracted the attention of our most enlightened and patriotic citizens, and that they are animated by a zeal for the extension of the silk culture which nothing short of a firm conviction of its great importance to the prosperity of the country could have excited.—We do trust, that at least the enterprising and wealthy farmers of Tennessee will without delay commence experiments, if only on a small scale, by which the value of the silk culture amongst us can be satisfactorily tested. Should it succeed to the extent which we confidently anticipate, those, who by their enterprise and public spirit, shall be the instruments of bringing it into general and extensive operation, will earn for themselves the proud title of the benefactors of their country—besides, that they will have greatly promoted their own individual pecuniary interest.

Ed. T. Far.

—

From the Farmer and Gardener.

SILK CULTURE.

The following remarks, on the culture of silk, and the propriety of introducing it into the Alms-house of Baltimore city and county, is most respectfully addressed to the favorable consideration of the Mayor and city council of Baltimore, the commissioners of Baltimore county, and the trustees for the Poor of said city and county by the Editor of the Farmer and Gardener, in the fond hope, that the suggestions thrown out may serve to bring into notice a branch of industry of incalculable value to the nation, and which, he also believes, if adopted and prosecuted with intelligence and energy at the Alms-house, would in a few years relieve the city and county from the entire burthen of the cost of its support

—

We insert, in the present number a very interesting and useful letter of Judge Spencer, of New York, on the subject of the cultivation of silk in this country. The facts to which he refers are both important and encouraging to such as have the means and disposition of entering into it. He estimates the net profits of twenty acres set in an orchard of mulberry at from $3,000 to $5,000 per annum. This, to those who have not particularly investigated the subject, may seem an exaggerated, if not startling sum. To us, however, it appears to be greatly under the amount which may, by judicious management, be realised from an orchard of twenty acres thus planted.

We are pleased with his suggestion, of adopting the culture of silk in Alms-houses, and have been, for several months, contemplating submitting a proposition to that effect to the trustees of the Alms-house of Baltimore city and county: having cursorily mentioned the subject to a gentleman recently a trustee, without entering into any particulars, early last fall; remarking—that we thought we had a plan in our mind, the which, when matured, we would submit to his consideration—a plan, by which, we thought, we would be able in a very few years, to make that establishment support itself. As our incessant occupation, has not hitherto afforded us the leisure to carry out our intentions, as then intimated, we will seize this, the first occasion which has presented itself, of so doing. It will now answer the two-fold purpose, of showing the practicability, we hope, of our views as then expressed, sanguine as they were, and of encouraging planters and farmers generally, throughout the country, (though it may fail of the other object, to turn their thoughts seriously to a proper consideration of the advantages and disadvantages which are likely to result from the proposed culture of the mulberry, management of the silk worm, and fabrication of silk. This is all we desire of them, being fully convinced that a dispassionate examination, must inevitably lead to such convictions of utility as cannot fail to raise up zealous friends in all directions.

From the facts stated by Judge Spencer, it appears, that silk worms have been raised in Windham county, Connecticut, ever since 1760, a period of seventy-five years; that during the last year, in the town of Mansfield, in the same state,

The fascination with silk was prompted in part by agricultural magazines that quite actively promoted a general awakening to new ideas about farming. The periodicals continually spoke about the detrimental impact of cotton, corn, and tobacco upon Tennessee's soil. Crop rotation, diversity of crops, and preserving the natural fertility of the soil were topics frequently appearing in the farm journals. Editors recommended the use of fertilizers, natural and commercial, to restore the worn-out soil and the planting of various grasses as alternative uses of the land. These magazines were likewise influential in stimulating interest in livestock production, especially the raising of sheep and production of wool. Mark Cockrill, a Davidson County farmer, quickly established himself as the leading authority on sheep raising. So successful was Cockrill that in 1854 at the World's Fair in London he won first prize for the finest wool in the world. No other Tennessee farmers received such recognition, but many of them turned increasingly to sheep, hog, and cattle production. Although some of their livestock was slaughtered and sent to out-of-state markets, the far greater quantity of the farmers' hogs, cattle, and mules—and sometimes poultry—was driven on foot from Tennessee to other states. Nashville and Knoxville became important centers of distribution for the livestock drovers.

For relief from the tedium of farming chores and for information as well, Tennessee farmers looked to the various agricultural organizations. Numerous such societies came into existence in the 1830s and 1840s, but the greatest accomplishments came in the 1850s. The legislature, upon the encouragement of Governor Andrew Johnson, established the State Board of Agriculture in 1854, which began sponsoring the creation of farmer organizations throughout the state and also funneled state funds to county societies and to sectional organizations founded in the three divisions of the state. The farmer groups devoted much of their attention and money (some said excessive) to staging county and divisional fairs, where information about farming techniques and implements could be shared while the large crowds in attendance socialized with neighbors and friends. With state financial aid, the divisional organizations in the eastern and western thirds of the state

---

Mark R. Cockrill brought international fame to Tennessee by his agricultural activities which were climaxed by the receipt of a prize for the finest wool in the world. From John Wooldridge, ed., *History of Nashville, Tenn.*

were able to purchase permanent fair sites at Knoxville and Jackson. Although the Middle Tennessee group never had permanent fair grounds, it nevertheless staged the most successful and elaborate of the divisional fairs. Beginning in 1855 and continuing through 1860, the crowning feature of the state organization was its promotion of the annual state agricultural fair, located in Nashville at a site purchased through the sale of state bonds. The fairs bore repeated testimony to the agricultural progress made by Tennessee in the antebellum decades, but the Civil War would severely disrupt farming activities as well as temporarily paralyze other major facets of the state's economic life.

A critical adjunct of Tennessee's flourishing agricultural economy was transportation—the ability to get the cash crops out of the state to the most desirable markets. The more the economy blossomed in the antebellum decades, the more inadequate became the old roads and the flatboats and keelboats on the rivers. In 1818 the first steamboat plied the Cumberland River, from the mouth of the river to Nashville, but a full ten years elapsed before a steamboat, the *Atlas,* successfully navigated the dangers of the Tennessee River to get to Knoxville. Until the coming of the railroads, the Cumberland and Mississippi rivers served as the main arteries of commercial transportation for the state. Blessed with such advantages, Middle and West Tennessee had little difficulty in providing agricultural products for interstate commerce. By 1850, for example, fifty-two steamboats made regular stops at Nashville. But what about East Tennessee? It most certainly had navigable rivers and passable roads within the region, but those stopped short of providing effective access to the adjoining states. When Captain S.D. Conner piloted the *Atlas* to Knoxville in 1828, some East Tennesseans believed the region to be on the verge of the fulfillment of a cherished dream of commercial ties with outside areas. The ceremony and jubilation that greeted Conner's arrival was partly in response to the notion that a new age of steamboat transportation was dawning, but one prominent Knoxvillian, Dr. J.G.M. Ramsey, punctured the high spirits by voicing another idea. Ramsey expressed grave doubts about the navigability of the Tennessee River and suggested that East Tennessee had best be thinking about railroads as the only feasible outlet for goods and products. Ramsey, though his outspoken opinion was resented by many fellow citizens, was right. Knoxville and East Tennessee never developed steamboat traffic except on a very minor scale.

In the early 1830s, a railroad fever swept across the state, and East Tennessee took the lead in urging railroad construction. In fact, in

Rogersville the first railroad promotional newspaper in the nation began its short-lived publication. West Tennesseans also quickly endorsed railroads as the best answer to the problem of getting cotton from the plantations to Memphis. Middle Tennessee, doing quite well as the economic and political leader of the state, showed only lukewarm interest at this time. In 1836 the legislature, yielding to pressures in behalf of governmental support of internal improvements, agreed that the state would underwrite one-third of the stock of qualified railroad and turnpike companies. The vote on this measure found East and West Tennessee heavily in favor and Middle Tennessee strongly opposed.

The 1836 law was ineffective, however, and Tennessee legislators two years later passed a new bill stipulating that the state would subscribe one-half of the stock of qualified railroad and turnpike companies up to a total of $3.7 million. This law also established a state bank (the one founded in 1820 had ceased operations in 1832) with an authorized capital of $5 million, part of which would come from the sale of bonds. The sectional alignments on this bill were the same as they had been in 1836—East and West Tennessee favoring and Middle Tennessee opposing. Ironically, the only region to benefit from the new law was Middle Tennessee, which received money for several turnpike projects. Because of the great difficulties of selling bonds and because of waning public enthusiasm, the General Assembly in 1840 repealed the parts of the 1838 law that extended aid to transportation companies. This action ushered in a hiatus of five or six years during which time little or nothing was done to build turnpikes or railroads.

Beginning in the late 1840s, however, there was a rejuvenated interest in railroads, and the legislature began chartering railroad companies with alacrity. In 1850 the state agreed to issue bonds up to $350,000 for the purchase of rails and equipment by the East Tennessee and Georgia Railroad Company. Two years later the process was regularized when the state decided to grant aid to railroad companies in the form of bonds, based on $8,000 per mile, to help pay for rails and equipment. With this kind of encouragement from the state government and with the capable leadership of various company officials, the railroad boom was on. In 1850 the state had not a single mile of operational railroad lines; in 1860 it had 1,200 miles.

But the bands of iron that annihilated time and space were not able to conquer Tennessee's sectionalism or, for the moment, its rugged topography. Almost without exception, the railroad lines followed north-south routes, each section of the state attempting to link itself with neighboring states rather than with another part of Tennessee. This arrangement reflected traditional beliefs that each section's best markets lay outside of the state, to the north or to the south, rather than within. As early as 1828 Dr. Ramsey had reminded his listeners that East Tennessee was "essentially an Atlantic country." And in West Tennessee, the first railroad completed there—the Memphis and Charleston line—also headed outside the state. An elaborate ceremony to mark this achievement took place in Memphis in the spring of 1857, when a barrel of water from the Atlantic was poured into the Mississippi River. The only direct connection between the state's sections was the Nashville and Chattanooga line, the first railroad to be completed in Tennessee. On the eve of the Civil War, a traveler still could not go by train directly from Knoxville to Nashville or from Nashville to Memphis. Although the state government poured thousands of dollars into railroad construction in the 1850s, it apparently never thought to devise or to insist upon a plan to create a network of rails that would bind together the state's three divisions.

Accompanying the economic development and political achievements of the antebellum era were a number of humanitarian reforms instigated by a small, determined group of crusaders. Even though Tennessee's efforts along these lines imitated reforms initiated elsewhere, mainly by northern and eastern states, the state can be credited nonetheless with some significant accomplishments. In 1832, for example, the legislature voted to establish a hospital for the insane, thereby committing the state government to be the agent solely responsible for the institutional care of the mentally ill. Governor William Carroll had championed this cause throughout his long tenure in office. Even so, construction of the mental institution proceeded with embarrassing slowness and considerable irresponsibility, and it was 1840 before the asylum was ready to receive its first patients in a still unfinished building in Nashville. A government report in 1847 noted that in the preceding two years the institution had admitted one hundred patients, of whom "2 escaped, when greatly improved." Although some citizens began to agitate for a better, more adequate facility as soon as the asylum opened, it took the late

---

(*Above*): The Hospital for the Insane, designed by Adolphus Heiman, was built at the urging of Dorothea Dix. (*Below*): Designed by William Strickland, the state capitol was completed in the mid-1850s. Illustrations from A.W. Putnam, *History of Middle Tennessee.*

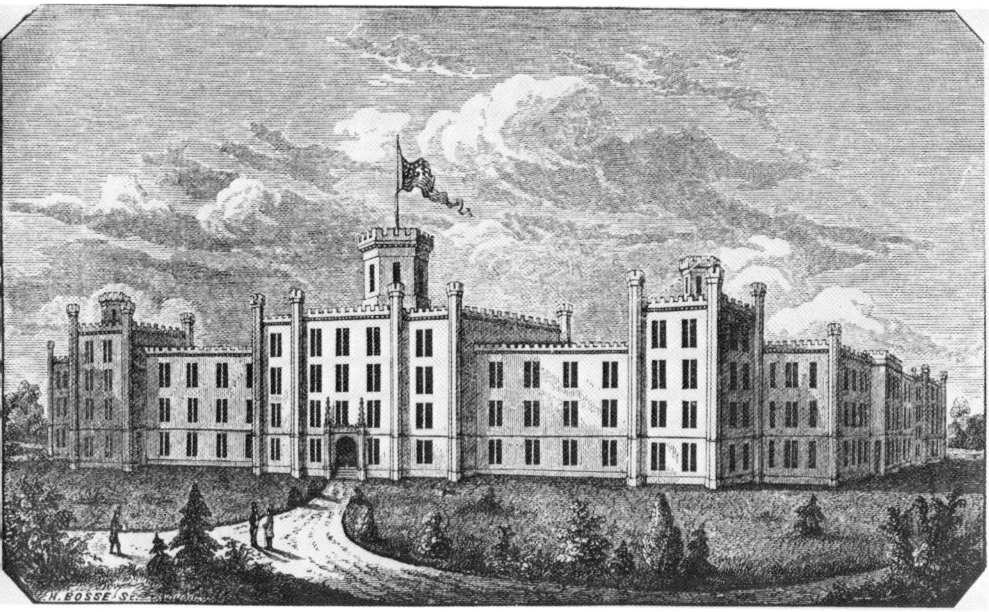

STATE CAPITOL, NASHVILLE, TENNESSEE.

1847 visit of the great national reformer, Dorothea Dix, to prod the legislature into action. In February of the following year the General Assembly endorsed Miss Dix's recommendations, which meant that the existing hospital must be abandoned and a new one constructed. After the initial wave of enthusiasm died down, however, hardly any progress was made on the new building, also located in Nashville. From 1852, when it finally received its first patients, until late 1859, the asylum admitted 577 persons and discharged 366 of them. Of those admitted, the overwhelming number of the men were farmers and laborers, whereas the majority of the women were farmers' wives and daughters.

Concurrent with these humanitarian interests were the efforts to revise the criminal code and to establish a state penitentiary. Throughout the 1820s Governor Carroll urged these measures upon a recalcitrant legislature, but it was 1829 before he succeeded in pushing through a bill embracing such reforms. The criminal law was changed so that only first-degree murder would be punishable by death. Other felonies would land the guilty in a state prison to be constructed at Nashville. The work on this new facility, modeled after prisons in the Northeast, began in the spring of 1830 and went so rapidly that the prison opened the following January. Within fifteen years or so, overcrowding became a perpetual problem at the penitentiary, although addition of cells in the 1850s afforded some relief. According to an 1859 report the prison population at that date was 378, consisting of 366 white males, 3 white females, 8 black males, and 1 black female. Nearly half of all the prisoners incarcerated from 1831 to 1859 were guilty of grand or petit larceny. Their major correctional activity was laboring in the prison's workshops, although some prisoners were used in the construction of the state capitol building when that project began. Basically, the idea of the penitentiary in that day was that it was a place of incarceration, not rehabilitation.

Some Tennessee reformers turned their energies to the field of education, hoping thereby to diminish the necessity for institutions such as prisons. Education went public in the antebellum years—but not without delays and difficulties. In the 1820s the state somewhat consistently and systematically set aside lands, the sale of which produced revenue for a common school fund. The first attempt to establish a public school system with this fund was made by the 1830 legislature, which distributed the total accumulation to the counties, to be managed by county commissioners for the support of schools. The plan was unsuccessful, however, and four years later the framers of the new state constitution prescribed a state board of commissioners (composed of the superintendent of public instruction, the treasurer, and the comptroller) to supervise the use of interest from the fund to finance public schools. But this plan was also discarded after the first superintendent of public instruction, Robert H. McEwen, was charged with mismanagement of the school monies entrusted to him. Consequently, the state bank eventually became responsible for handling all financial transactions relative to the school fund, and for several years the interest earned (about $100,000 per year) was the main support provided by the state for the public schools. Finally, in 1854, upon the strong urging of Governor Andrew Johnson, the legislature enacted a tax for the direct support of public education. By the end of the 1850s the revenue generated by this tax had helped swell the common school fund to an endowment of $1.5 million, from which more than $200,000 was allocated annually to the public schools, at that time enrolling approximately 140,000 students. The establishment of a public school system was a major milestone of the antebellum period, but private academies and colleges also grew in number and frequently in enhanced quality during this same period. The house of pre-Civil War reform had many rooms, but hardly a more important one than education.

Taken as a whole, these maturing years of growth and development were characterized by boundless optimism—at least on the part of white Tennesseans. But as 1860 approached, the national debates over the extension and preservation of slavery aroused an uneasy feeling that the days of economic progress, political achievement, and social reform were coming to an end, to be halted by the disturbing issue that seemed to have no solution agreeable to all parts of the Union. Those Tennesseans who harbored such apprehensions were to have their worst fears confirmed very shortly.

3. A Time of Testing, 1860–1900

The Preacher in Ecclesiastes declared: "To every thing there is a season and a time to every purpose under the heaven . . . . A time to kill, and a time to heal; a time to break down, and a time to build up." This ancient maxim seems well suited to describe Tennessee's history, as well as that of the United States, in the second half of the nineteenth century. The years from 1860 to 1900 were Tennessee's time of testing as it coped with armed conflict and death and devastation, with uncertainty and tension resulting from reconstruction, and with recovery and readjustment in the last three decades of the century.

The election of Lincoln to the presidency in 1860 was the catalyst that provoked secession and rebellion by the Southern states. That Lincoln and the Republican party did not appear on the ballots in the Southern states constituted evidence of worsening sectional hostility. With the heavy Democratic vote in Tennessee split between John C. Breckinridge (Southern Democrat) and Stephen A. Douglas (Northern Democrat), the state gave a plurality (47.6 percent) of its vote to John Bell, longtime and prominent Tennessee politician, who sought the presidency on the ticket of the newly formed Constitutional Union party. Although Lincoln had no support in the state, Tennessee was not particularly perturbed by his election, most of the influential state leaders counseling a wait-and-see attitude. But not so in other states of the South. With South Carolina in the vanguard, the secession movement became an undeniable reality in December 1860.

Governor Isham Harris, a powerful representative of the states-rights element in Tennessee, was not content to wait while other slave states withdrew from the Union. He called a special session of the General Assembly in January 1861, at which he urged that a state convention be held to determine Tennessee's course of action. The legislature considered the matter but stipulated that the voters should decide in a February referendum whether a convention would be called. When that date arrived, seven states had already seceded from the Union and were at that moment meeting in Montgomery to establish the provisional government of the Confederacy. At the polls in Tennessee, 54.5 percent of the 127,200 voters opposed the call for a state convention. West Tennessee was the only section to favor the convention (74 percent); East Tennessee overwhelmingly rejected the convention proposal (81 percent); while Middle Tennessee reported an uncomfortable division—51 percent opposed the convention call. Without question, Tennesseans' devotion to the Union held the upper hand in this first significant test.

Four months later, however, the situation was dramatically reversed. At a special session in the spring, the General Assembly adopted a "Declaration of Independence" which if accepted by the voters would place Tennessee outside the Union but, technically speaking, not in the Confederacy. The legislators designated June 8 as the date for a plebiscite on the declaration. By that time Tennessee, for all practical purposes, was already out of the Union, and hence the voters were simply being asked to ratify a *fait accompli.* Significantly, 152,000 voters participated in the June referendum—25,000 more than had voted in February and 7,000 more than had voted in the presidential election the year before—demonstrating the intensity of feeling in the state. This time, 69 percent of those going to the polls voted for separation from the Union. Approximately the same percentage of East Tennessee votes were cast *against* separation, but West Tennessee, as expected, returned a heavy vote (82 percent) in behalf of separation. The most remarkable transformation occurred in Middle Tennessee, which gave 88 percent of its vote to the separation cause. In June, Tennessee thus left the Union—the last of the Southern states to do so.

The dramatic shift toward secession had occurred quickly. The Fort Sumter attack in South Carolina in April and Lincoln's subsequent call for troops had erased whatever lingering doubts Tennesseans might have had about the possibility of a North-South war. Furthermore, Governor Harris, a demagogic leader with unshakable convictions about the state's destiny in the Confederacy, overpowered those who disagreed with him. Weeks before the June referendum, Harris concluded a military pact with the Confederacy and then set about raising troops. In the absolutely crucial area of Middle Tennessee the impact of these developments steadily diminished Unionist sentiment.

East Tennessee, of course, continued to favor the Union. Although there were pockets of secessionist support in the region, the great majority of the people steadfastly refused to condone Tennessee's departure from the Union. Two bitter political foes, Andrew Johnson and Thomas A.R. Nelson, laid aside their earlier antagonisms to conduct a joint speaking tour of East Tennessee, urging a rejection of secession at the forthcoming referendum in June. They were joined by several other political leaders who called for a convention to meet in Knoxville in late May. Out of this meeting came a firm resolve to oppose Tennessee's separation. But since the statewide vote subsequently went against the wishes of East Tennessee Unionists, they held a second convention, at Greeneville, about ten days following the plebiscite. The Greeneville delegates concluded their somewhat stormy meeting by taking a drastic step: they asked the General Assembly for permission to separate East Tennessee from the rest of the state. Their petition was tolerantly received by the legislature in mid-summer but was not acted upon.

Eight months later, the first blows of the Civil War were felt in Tennessee. On extremely cold days in mid-February 1862, Federal naval and land forces attacked Forts Henry and Donelson (on the Tennessee and Cumberland rivers, respectively), brought a swift end to the bungling Confederate defense of the forts, and then moved immediately up the Cumberland River to occupy a panic-stricken Nashville. The attack upon and collapse of the two forts indicated the crucial and difficult role Tennessee would play in nearly four years of armed strife. Geography dictated that the state's special location in the Upper South, along with its river system, would make Tennessee a great thoroughfare for invading Federal armies bent on clearing the way for the conquest of the Deep South. And when the sounds of the last firing guns were silenced, Tennessee had been the scene of more military engagements than any other state except Virginia.

The quick surrender of Forts Henry and Donelson reflected the woefully inadequate preparations made to defend Tennessee as well as the warped overall military strategy carried out in 1861. When General Leonidas Polk arrived in Tennessee in July to take command of Confederate forces, he inherited a sizable (at least on paper) but poorly equipped state army recruited by Governor Harris and General Gideon J. Pillow. Polk readily agreed with their plan to make the Mississippi River the major line of defense for Tennessee, since he shared their conviction that the initial Federal attacks would proceed down the Mississippi River and that Kentucky's declaration of neutrality would prevent Union troops from invading Tennessee via that state. Accordingly, construction was begun in the summer on various forts along the Mississippi River—to the neglect of the rest of the state.

General Polk was succeeded in September by Albert Sidney Johnston, who took charge of the military department which included all of Tennessee. By the time of Johnston's arrival in the state, Polk and Pillow had already pushed the so-called western flank into Kentucky by seizing the Mississippi River town of Columbus in early September. Then when Johnston looked at the meager East Tennessee defenses, he saw that Confederate General Felix Zollicoffer had already maneuvered his line of troops to the Cumberland Gap area. Thus, in Johnston's estimation, Nashville was too far south of the eastern and western defense lines to make it the logical defense area for the central portion of the state. Consequently, he elected to push the center line to Bowling Green, Kentucky, some sixty miles northeast of Nashville. Because of these activities and misplaced strategies, little attention was directed to the protection of such natural avenues as the Cumberland and Tennessee rivers or to the alarming vulnerability of the city of Nashville. General U.S. Grant's rapid movement from Fort Donelson to Nashville was not only testimony of his prowess as a commander, but equally important, it was a disturbing commentary on Confederate defense preparations.

As Federal soldiers approached Nashville, General Johnston hastily evacuated his troops, taking them to Corinth, Mississippi. There Johnston was joined by Rebel forces commanded by Generals P.G.T. Beauregard and Braxton Bragg. Shortly, the three generals decided to settle the score with Grant and General William T. Sherman by attacking them near Savannah, Tennessee. The battle of Shiloh (named for the church nearby) began in early April with most of the advantages on the side of the Confederates. They had managed, for example, to catch Grant and his troops completely by surprise. Despite successes in early skirmishing, however, the Confederate attack became mired in confusion and delay, especially after a stray bullet lodged in General Johnston's thigh during the first day of battle and ended his life. General Grant, aided by the arrival of 30,000 reinforcements the next day, went on the offensive and routed the Confederates, who were understandably eager to obey Beauregard's orders to retreat to Corinth. The tremendous losses, on both sides, made the Shiloh campaign one of the bloodiest of the entire Civil War.

The results of the engagements at Forts Henry and Donelson and Shiloh and the Federal occupation of Nashville and then Memphis (June 1862) meant that Middle and West Tennessee early fell under Union domination. Yet the daring Confederate cavalry raids of John Hunt Morgan and Nathan Bedford Forrest challenged Federal control of the region from time to time, especially in the summer and autumn of 1862. Forrest's capture of General Don Carlos Buell's brigade at Murfreesboro was one of the highlights of Confederate retaliation in Middle Tennessee. But the apparent showdown between Confederate and Federal troops in that part of the state occurred at Stone's River (Murfreesboro) in a three-day engagement bridging December and January. General Bragg, commanding the Army of Tennessee, had retreated to Murfreesboro after a discouraging foray into Kentucky. When Union General William Rosecrans, commander at Nashville, learned of Bragg's movement into Rutherford County, he determined to drive Bragg out. The fighting began on New Year's Eve of 1862 and went so well for the Confederates that Bragg telegraphed a message to President Jefferson Davis the following day, assuring him, "God has granted us a happy New Year." But victory eluded Bragg, as it often did, for Rosecrans received timely reinforcements and compelled Bragg to retreat toward Chattanooga on January 3.

No further major battles took place in Middle and West Tennessee until the waning months of the war, when General John Bell Hood launched a futile Confederate invasion of the middle section of the state. Having escaped from the trauma of Sherman's ruthless attacks in Georgia, Hood had removed his Army of Tennessee from that state and had then transported them across northern Alabama and on into Tennessee. His first serious engagement took place in November 1864 at Franklin, where he successfully drove the Federals from the field—but at the cost of more than 6,000 Rebels dead and wounded. Hood then recklessly determined to take his fight all the way to Nashville, an impossible goal considering both his small number of troops in comparison to the Union army and the formidable ring of defenses surrounding Nashville. The two armies clashed in mid-December and Hood's troops were quickly sent reeling back into a hasty retreat. Retracing their steps south through Middle Tennessee, Hood and his men left the state about as suddenly as they had arrived.

Meanwhile, East Tennessee, in the eyes of the Richmond and Washington governments, had served in many respects as a separate and distinct theater of war. Confederate domination in that region, albeit uneasy, was established early in the war by a small band of soldiers dispatched to East Tennessee by Governor Harris and General Pillow. Ironically, the strongest pro-Union part of Tennessee was thus under Confederate control from the outset. This irony was not lost on the people of the region who experienced the pangs of divided loyalties more than did any other part of the state—or the South as a whole. Families were split and friendships severed, churches were divided, and some able-bodied young men rushed to join Yankee troops while others enlisted in the Rebel army. Although there were no major battles in the region until the autumn of 1863, East Tennessee was a land daily torn by guerilla activity, bushwhackers, military raids, and a profound disruption of social and economic life. Initially Confederate troops in East Tennessee were somewhat conciliatory toward the local citizenry, but after a bridge-burning episode in the fall of 1861 the Rebel officers clamped down. Unionist sympathizers had hatched a scheme to dynamite various railroad bridges in the region in order to cripple Confederate transportation lines. They had been assured that Federal troops, which were to invade from Kentucky, would rush to support them and other loyal Unionists in East Tennessee. But even though the courageous bridge-burners carried out their mission, no Yankee troops arrived—the result of shifting military strategies by Union generals who had decided to hit Middle Tennessee instead.

National attention, north and south, focused on East Tennessee in 1863, when campaigns at Chattanooga and Knoxville took place. The Chattanooga engagement followed a disastrous defeat of Rosecrans' Union troops in September at Chickamauga—an impressive victory for General Bragg. Rosecrans then retreated into Chattanooga. Bragg had an excellent chance to polish off the enemy, but instead he stalled and dispersed his troops and elected to lay siege to Chattanooga. In late November, when Union forces commanded by Grant, who had replaced Rosecrans, decided to lift Bragg's prolonged siege of Chattanooga, they were able to carry out their attack upon the Rebels effectively and successfully. Bragg's men in fact fled in panic into Georgia, making Chattanooga another trophy on the shelf of Grant's victories.

The chances for Yankee success at Chattanooga were enhanced by Bragg's decision to detach General James Longstreet and send him north to Knoxville, a city occupied in September by Federal troops under General Ambrose Burnside. Longstreet and his soldiers left the Chattanooga area in early November to move up the Tennessee River valley toward Knoxville. After a series of skirmishes in the Knoxville vicinity, General Burnside shrewdly drew Longstreet into the city where the Rebels had to go against strong defense fortifications. By the end of November (shortly after Bragg's defeat at Chattanooga), Longstreet's men had been driven out of Knoxville, to retreat into upper East Tennessee and eventually Virginia. With Union triumphs at both Chattanooga and Knoxville, East Tennessee was at long last liberated—though not spared further military activity which continued in the region until 1865.

While battles, skirmishes, and raids made headlines across Tennessee, another story unfolded—the military governorship of Andrew Johnson. Appointed by President Lincoln, Johnson arrived in Nashville in March 1862 with the avowed purpose of steering Tennessee back into the Union as quickly as possible. His heavy-handed and ruthless tactics in Nashville—censorship of the press, shutting down publishing houses, imprisonment of the mayor and certain clergymen—brought him the unrelenting enmity of Middle and West Tennesseans. But whatever his faults, Johnson seemed genuinely intent on restoring his state to the Union. Two months after Johnson assumed office, a small group of Unionists met in Nashville to declare publicly their support of Johnson's goal of readmission for Tennessee. Later that same year Johnson reasoned that he might stimulate the desire for restoration to the Union by staging congressional elections in the two West Tennessee districts—an area noted for secessionist and Confederate leanings. But because of continuing military activity in the region, only one of the districts was actually able to hold an election. Its victorious candidate, however, was denied a seat in Congress by political leaders not willing to give Tennessee such easy access to the nation's capital while the state was still legally in rebellion. Johnson suffered another setback when his plans to cultivate and nurture Unionist support throughout the state were upset to some degree by Lincoln's Emancipation Proclamation of January 1863. Although Lincoln specifically exempted Tennessee from the Proclamation's provisions, the document nonetheless contributed to a split among the state's Unionists. One wing, led by Johnson himself, favored the abolition of slavery, whereas the opposing group wanted readmission to the Union with slavery intact.

Differences within the Unionist camp became increasingly apparent. In the summer of 1863, for example, hopes for a gubernatorial election as a first step toward Tennessee's re-entry into the Union were dashed

---

(*Left*): Andrew Johnson was "millitary governor" during the Civil War. He is shown here as President. (*Right*): William G. Brownlow, the Reconstruction governor, prevented ex-Confederates from voting and from public office, while allowing blacks to vote. Photographs courtesy Library of Congress.

when Johnson, disturbed by internal bickering among the Unionists, refused to call such an election. But the more conservative Unionists staged a somewhat farcical gubernatorial election anyway, in which William B. Campbell was the winner. They then sent an emissary to President Lincoln to plead that he accept Campbell as the duly elected governor. But the President refused, choosing instead to continue his support of Andrew Johnson. Meanwhile, Confederate sympathizers in the lower part of Middle Tennessee had held an election in which they chose Robert L. Caruthers as governor. Naturally he was not recognized or accepted as the state's chief executive.

The presidential election of 1864 served as an opportunity for each of the Unionist factions to test its strength. The more conservative (anti-Johnson) element threw its support to the Democratic party's candidate, General George McClellan, while the other group backed the Republican (Union) ticket of Lincoln and Johnson. In late September, Johnson issued a proclamation requiring that every prospective voter take an oath that he would not support a negotiated peace with the Confederacy—which was the main plank of the Democratic platform. As one newspaper editor aptly observed: "Andy will let us vote, if we swear to vote for him—not otherwise." Needless to say, election day brought victory to the Lincoln-Johnson slate in Tennessee. Congress refused to recognize the votes from this election, however, because Tennessee was an area still in a rebellious condition.

Shortly after the November election, Tennessee Unionists called for a state convention for the purpose of taking specific steps to restore the state to the Union. Although inclement weather and Hood's attack upon Nashville caused the meeting to be postponed for a month, about five hundred delegates, some elected, some self-appointed, assembled in Nashville in January 1865.

With Johnson's blessing, this convention proceeded to make decisions that launched the reconstruction period in Tennessee. That the assembly lacked legal authority or foundation bothered some of the delegates who soon left town; but others stayed, arguing that the restoration process had to start somewhere. The convention agreed to ask the voters, in a referendum set for February, to amend the 1835 state constitution to abolish slavery and also to approve a series of resolutions: all actions of the state government after May 1861 (the date of Tennessee's military league with the Confederacy) were to be voided; gubernatorial and legislative elections would be held in March; and the legislature elected then would establish qualifications for voters. The convention next named a slate of candidates, headed by William G. Brownlow for governor, for the March elections and declared that the only persons eligible to vote in the February referendum and March elections would be those who had been entitled to vote in the 1864 presidential contest—which would effectively disqualify Confederate sympathizers. It was clear from the outset that the matter of suffrage would be of paramount concern throughout the days of the reconstruction experience.

In February the voters accepted the constitutional amendment, as well as the resolutions; then in March they approved the candidates offered by the January convention. In both February and March the vote was very small, approximately 25,000, with no more than half the state's counties participating—a reminder of the chaotic conditions still prevailing in much of the state (absence of local governments, disrupted transportation and communication, and sporadic Confederate raids). There was certainly no ground swell of popular support for the actions of the January convention, but the votes in both instances did meet the 10 percent requirement established by President Lincoln's amnesty proclamation and were therefore valid. Accordingly, in early April the newly elected legislators and governor met in Nashville. Brownlow, the fiery Unionist newspaper editor from Knoxville, was inaugurated on April 5—four days before General Lee's surrender to Grant at Appomattox Courthouse and ten days before President Lincoln's assassination.

For at least the next two years, the question of who should have the right to vote was the all-consuming problem of the Brownlow government. Since only those with impeccable Unionist credentials occupied legislative seats and the governor's office, their determination to prohibit ex-Confederates from voting was expected. The first franchise law, passed in June 1865, effectively accomplished this by setting up six categories of eligibility—all of which ruled out the Rebels. Moreover, for the first time in the state's history, voter registration (to be handled by county court clerks) was prescribed. The initial test of the franchise law occurred in August, when congressional elections were held in the state's eight districts. But Brownlow's candidates carried only three districts—a quite disappointing show of strength, in the eyes of the governor. He therefore tampered with the election returns in one of the districts, capriciously counting some clearly illegal ballots while throwing out some legitimate ones, and thereby added another one of his candidates to the victory column. The summer's election jolted Brownlow into the realization that his followers, the "radicals" (so designated because they subscribed to the harsh program of Reconstruction advocated by congressional radicals), did not enjoy widespread support, even among Unionists. Whereupon the governor insisted upon an even stricter franchise law as an effective means of establishing his political control of the state. In the spring of 1866, the General Assembly finally passed such a law, authorizing the governor to appoint special commissioners in every county to supervise voter registration.

Brownlow feared, however, that in time even this new voting law might not be enough to keep him and his radical friends in office. With an eye focused on the forthcoming 1867 state elections, Brownlow therefore embarked upon one of his most controversial missions: to give black men the right to vote. A triumphal trip to the Southern Loyalist Convention in Philadelphia and a speaking tour of Northern cities fired the governor's determination to push black suffrage. The Tennessee legislature reluctantly but obediently heeded Brownlow's call and approved black suffrage in February 1867. Tennessee thus endorsed black franchise a full two years before Congress passed the Fifteenth Amendment and three years before the states finally ratified that amendment.

One of the major goals of Brownlow and his followers was to get Tennessee readmitted to the Union as quickly as possible. Approaching the task of restoration in the spring of 1865, Brownlow urged quick approval of the Thirteenth Amendment to the U.S. Constitution that eliminated slavery throughout the nation. The legislature complied by ratifying the amendment without opposition, then chose two U.S. senators, David Patterson and Joseph Fowler, and called for congressional elections in August. When these elected officials went to Washington in December 1865, they confidently expected to claim seats in Congress. But a serious battle developing between Congress and President Johnson over the matter of bringing the Southern states back into the Union was to delay their acceptance for several months.

Eventually, after congressional radicals decreed that ratification of the Fourteenth Amendment (citizenship rights for Negroes) was a prerequisite for readmission, Governor Brownlow convened a special session of the legislature in July 1866 to approve it. The state senate ratified the amendment easily, despite mounting sentiment in Tennessee against it, but in the lower house there was a concerted effort by "conservative" members to prevent a vote by making sure a quorum was not present. Their obstructive tactics were futile, however, because Brownlow's leaders had two house members arrested and hauled to Nashville, where the two legislators were imprisoned in a room adjoining the legislative chamber and actually counted as present but not voting. Before the month ended, the General Assembly ratified the Fourteenth Amendment, making Tennessee the third state in the entire nation to give its approval and paving the way for its readmission to the Union shortly thereafter. Tennessee thus became the first of the Confederate states to rejoin the Union, a goal sought since 1862.

Once Tennessee was safely back in the Union, the question of who should rule in the state became even more critical. Brownlow fervently desired reelection in 1867, but he met a determined challenge from Emerson Etheridge, the candidate of the conservative Unionists. This group increasingly resented Brownlow's autocratic rule and believed that the voting franchise should be opened to at least some ex-Confederates. But for the moment both competitors courted the black vote in the vicious and bitter gubernatorial campaign. Altogether more than 96,000 voted in this election, with perhaps as many as 40,000 being newly enfranchised black voters. Thanks to this heavy turnout by blacks, Brownlow won easily over Etheridge, and his followers captured all of the congressional seats and almost all of the General Assembly posts.

Such a resounding victory gave new impetus to the efforts of certain dissident elements to bring down the house of radicalism. They established organizations such as the Knights of the White Camellia, the Council of Safety, and the White Brotherhood, but the most important was the Ku Klux Klan, organized in Pulaski in late 1865. Although seemingly nothing more than a social club at first, the Klan, believing the key to political control to be the curtailment of the black vote, soon became a militant organization with General Nathan Bedford Forrest as "Grand Wizard of the Empire." The Klan's activities, designed to harass and intimidate blacks—especially the potential voters among them—increased steadily in Middle and West Tennessee, to the point that the General Assembly passed special legislation providing penalties for those participating in the Klan. Eventually Brownlow hired a Cincinnati detective, Seymour Barmore, to infiltrate the Klan to learn the identity of its principal leaders. But Barmore's bullet-pierced body was pulled from the bottom of the Duck River shortly thereafter—grim testimony of the lawless group's vow to disrupt radical control of Tennessee.

Swiftly but without violence radical domination came to an end in 1869 when ex-Confederates finally gained the right to vote. Early that year Brownlow had concluded his four years of iron rule as governor by departing from the state to take a seat in the U.S. Senate. His successor, State Senate Speaker DeWitt Senter, was a radical also but was not inclined to imitate Brownlow's oppressive control. Shortly after assuming office, Senter faced a gubernatorial contest, and when a schism developed within the radical camp as the election neared, he got the jump on his rival contender, fellow radical William B. Stokes, by declaring himself in favor of universal manhood suffrage in the state. Senter then proceeded to appoint new commissioners of voter registration, ousting those who would have denied the former Rebels a vote. Senter's election was assured as 175,000 voters marched to the polls. He carried all three sections of the state, and in Middle and West Tennessee the newly enfranchised white voters helped give him overwhelming majorities. Although defeated candidate Stokes cried fraud and pleaded with President Grant to intervene and overturn the election results, the President refused. The cause of radicalism was doomed.

With the suffrage doors now open to ex-Confederates, they and other conservatives gained domination of the legislature convening in the fall of 1869 and immediately set about dismantling much of the reconstruction program enacted by the radicals. To ensure the continuance of conservative control of state government, the General Assembly called for a constitutional convention. It assembled in January 1870 and within six weeks had drafted a new constitution—one that, with amendments, remains today as the state's governing document. The most controversial question was the familiar one: who should have the right to vote? Ex-Rebels were now secure in their newly-won suffrage, but the voting rights of blacks was a matter still hotly contested. A majority of the delegates finally consented to black suffrage, but not before writing a significant requirement into the suffrage clause: "each voter shall give . . . satisfactory evidence that he has paid the poll taxes assessed against him . . . ." Although public schools were to benefit from the revenue produced by this new tax, and though the tax was a voting obstacle to all low-income groups, white or black, many delegates saw it primarily as a means of disenfranchising blacks. And blacks apparently read the same ulterior purpose into the tax clause, for most of them opposed the 1870 constitution when the state at large ratified it by a 3 to 1 margin.

In the November election of that year Tennessee voters overwhelmingly elected Democrat (conservative) John C. Brown as governor, chose Democrats for six of the eight congressional seats, and sent large Democratic majorities to both houses of the legislature. The state had now shifted from Brownlow and radical rule to the opposite, for the new governor had been a major general in the Confederate army and a member of the Ku Klux Klan.

Thus the decade of tragedy and trauma ended. Fortunately for Tennessee, it never again experienced a time of testing equivalent to that of the 1860s. Tennesseans, showing remarkable resilience, quickly turned from the travail of that decade to face the challenge of recovery and readjustment. The following thirty years bore out the scriptural description —"a time to heal . . . and a time to build up."

The phenomenal growth of manufacturing and industry in the state during the post-1870 period furnished ample evidence of this building process. Although the nationwide Panic of 1873 crippled the industrial expansion that had begun even in the midst of the turmoil of the 1860s, the decade of the 1880s marked a great boom period for this sector of the economy, thanks in large measure to the rapidly expanding coal and iron industries in Tennessee. By 1890, the total value of manufactured goods had reached $72 million—almost twice the value reported ten years earlier. For the first time in the state's history, the value of manufactured goods had exceeded the total worth of farm products. Even so, despite these tremendous strides made in a relatively short period, the industrial lead was only temporary. Tennessee's economy was still primarily agricultural, for in 1900 the total value of farm products once again surpassed that of manufactured goods.

Equally remarkable in the story of economic recovery is the fact that Tennesseans accomplished most of it with their own resources and by virtue of their own diligence. The commonly-held notion of Northern capital rushing in to rebuild the South is not generally applicable to Tennessee. Except for the iron industry in Chattanooga, there are few important examples of out-of-state investors pumping money into the state's burgeoning industrial system.

Tennessee agriculture suffered much more from the Civil War than did the industrial sector, and recovery was slower. For example, the total value of farm property in 1870 had dropped more than 17 percent below the 1860 figure of $340 million, and the 1860 total was not matched again until 1900. The value of farm products also declined, experiencing a devastating drop of nearly $31 million in value during the twenty years following 1870, when it had peaked at $86.4 million. The plummeting prices of farm products (especially cotton) on the national market were mainly responsible for this discouraging agricultural showing. Luckily for the farmers and the state's economy as a whole, the agricultural sector pulled out of its tailspin in the 1890s and was expanding again by 1900. Whether the farm economy was prospering or depressed in this post-1870 period, however, the overwhelming majority of Tennesseans remained either employed or otherwise directly connected with agricultural productivity.

Creating disquiet in the economic sphere was the financial condition of the state government itself. Most of the attention focused on the bonded indebtedness which by 1870 had reached $43 million, second highest state debt in the entire nation. Almost all of the debt had grown out of the state government's financial assistance to railroads, first during the 1850s and then during the Brownlow administration in the 1860s. The revelation of corruption and scandal connected with railroad bonds issued during the Brownlow regime caused some Tennessee leaders to insist that the bonds were fraudulent and should therefore not be honored by the state. The nagging debt problem quickly became as much a political matter as an economic one.

Throughout the decade of the 1870s a succession of Democratic governors presented proposals to fund the state debt, but the legislature's decision in 1873 to fund the debt at face value with new bonds bearing 6 percent interest was the only plan accepted until nine years later. Many different plans were advanced during the interim. The state's voters rejected one proposal in a statewide referendum in 1879, the state supreme court struck down another plan that was enacted by a Republican administration in 1881, and still another Republican proposal was repealed when the Democrats came back into power in 1883. The Democrats' own plan, which represented a final resolution of the debt controversy, provided that the state would issue thirty-year bonds to fund $26 million of the debt at fifty cents on the dollar and would pay the remaining $3 million of the debt at full value.

The public's confidence in its government was further shaken, shortly before the final debt-retirement plan was approved, when the state treasurer, Marshall T. Polk, left town suddenly and mysteriously. A subsequent audit showed a deficiency in his office of slightly more than $374,000 (a portion of which was later recovered). Polk was captured near the Mexican border within a few weeks of his disappearance, and this favorite nephew of the late President James K. Polk spent his remaining days in prison, until his death in the spring of 1884.

While most of the state struggled to get back on its feet economically, the city of Memphis wrestled with mosquitoes and yellow fever. Memphis had never been a healthy place to live, its mortality rate being the highest of eleven major cities in the nation according to an 1872 report, but in the space of six years during the 1870s three separate yellow fever epidemics swept through the city. In that decade of rebuilding and new growth for Southern cities, Memphis was the exception—it lost population (40,200 in 1870; 33,600 in 1880). On the eve of the 1873 epidemic, a book about Memphis was published in which the author boasted: "I honestly believe Memphis to be the healthiest place on the river from the mouth of the Ohio down." The death of 2,000 persons during September and October gave a hollow sound to the author's claim for Memphis as "the healthiest place." Five years later a much more severe plague hit the city, when 5,150 persons died as victims of yellow fever. During the frightful months of this epidemic, there was a frenzied exodus of nearly 25,000 inhabitants who fled the cursed city, leaving behind approximately 20,000 to nurse the sick, bury the dead, or become the mosquito's next victim. In 1879 the third outbreak, a much milder one, accounted for 600 deaths. Never once suspecting the mosquito as the villain, Memphians naturally did not take proper preventive measures during these traumatic events of the 1870s. Instead, superstition prevailed as people doused themselves with cologne and rosewater or wore onions on their clothing—actions believed capable of warding off the dread disease.

Indeed, even the Civil War did not have the devastating impact upon Memphis that yellow fever did. One historian has aptly noted that 1880, not 1860, was the critical year in the city's history. Not only did Memphis lose population during the 1870s, but its financial situation became so intolerable that in 1879 the city surrendered its charter and temporarily went out of existence. For the next ten years the state of Tennessee governed Memphis as a special taxing district, during which time the state helped the city restore and rebuild itself. A new Memphis arose after 1880, thanks to the sanitation and public health revolution, prompted by the state, that took place there in the last two decades of the nineteenth century. Memphis again became a desirable and pleasant place to live, its population nearly doubling in the ten years after 1880.

In the post-Reconstruction decades Tennessee's efforts to diversify and strengthen its agriculture while promoting increased industrialization placed the state squarely behind advocates of the "New South" spirit in the economic realm. Similarly, Tennessee's politics more often than not conformed to patterns associated with the New South era, namely, domination by the Democratic party. But the state's Democrats learned that the threat of Republican power was serious and persistent. In fact, in 1872, just two short years after the redemption of the state by the Democrats, Republicans made a formidable showing in all the state races and, aided by a coalition of independent Democrats, gained control of the General Assembly. This surprising Republican strength helped turn the state elections two years later into a bitter and violent struggle by both parties to establish control of the statewide political system. But on election day the Democrats swept everything in sight and dominated state politics for the remainder of the century.

The Republicans bounced back, however, on two subsequent occasions. Because the Democrats were badly divided over the funding of the state debt, Republicans were able to win the governor's race in 1880. Fourteen years later, they waged a vigorous gubernatorial campaign, hoping to capitalize on widespread anti-Democratic feeling generated by a national depression that was blamed on the Democratic administration in Washington. When the election results were made known publicly (about four or five weeks after election day), they showed that Republican Henry Clay Evans had defeated the Democratic incumbent, Peter Turney. Evans never served as governor, however, because the legislature set up a committee to investigate the election and to recount the ballots. The Democratic-controlled General Assembly reached the not unexpected conclusion that Turney had actually won, and he was inaugurated in May 1895.

In addition to the continuing challenge from Republicans, Tennessee Democrats experienced internal problems. In the latter decades of the nineteenth century, the Democratic camp was divided into three recognizable groups. The Bourbon Democrats were the states rights, conservative element in the party, whereas the New South Democrats were the more progressive, economic development faction. Generally, these two wings were the chief rivals for control of the party, but beginning in the mid-1880s a third group of Democrats, the rural, "plain folk" segment (frequently called the "wool hat boys"), flexed its political muscle. Its first real opportunity came in 1886, when it succeeded in getting Robert L. Taylor nominated at the Democratic state convention, an accomplishment that was duplicated two years later.

The 1886 campaign was fascinating not only because of Taylor's emergence as the spokesman for the usually voiceless third Democratic group, but also because the Republicans nominated Taylor's older brother, Alfred, as their gubernatorial contender. This set the stage for the so-called "War of the Roses," the state Republicans having chosen the red rose and the Democrats the white rose as their symbols. It was a fraternal conflict that captured the imagination and attention of the general public in Tennessee and elsewhere as well. As they traveled together and ate together, the brothers conducted forty-one joint debates throughout the state in September and October. The brothers were superb platform performers—fiddling, singing, and swapping anecdotes—and their visits to the various towns caused thousands to turn out to greet them. At one of the campaign stops, Bob Taylor impishly gave his brother's speech—much to the delight of the crowd but to the dismay of Alf, who was forced to deliver an impromptu speech to an amused audience. The Taylor brothers' campaign doubtless gave the public a pleasant, entertaining interlude—a sort of escape from the problems that had troubled the state. By early November, the Republican and Democratic roses were beginning to wilt as the voters rendered their decision. They handed Bob a victory by 16,000 votes; Alf would have to wait thirty-four years before becoming governor.

The "plain folk" element continued to exert political influence in the 1890s, but in ways somewhat different from the previous decade. About the time of Taylor's victory, new farmers' organizations began to spring up in Tennessee, much as they were doing in other states. They were not directly interested in politics at first, however; instead they addressed themselves to the worsening economic situation of farmers in the 1880s. By the end of that decade, the Agricultural Wheel organization claimed about 78,000 members in Tennessee, the highest number of any state, and the Farmers' Alliance meanwhile had 20,000 members, mostly concentrated in Middle Tennessee. These two groups merged in 1889 as the Farmers' and Laborers' Union (popularly called the Alliance) and chose John P. Buchanan as president. The following year the Alliance people, with Buchanan as their candidate for governor, went to the Democratic state convention determined to control the nomination, as had been done in a less organized way in 1886, and they succeeded. Buchanan carried the Democratic party to victory, though the New South and Bourbon leaders exhibited no fondness for him and immediately began efforts to head off his nomination for re-election in 1892.

By the time that election year arrived, a new party—the People's (or Populist) party—had appeared throughout the nation, including Tennessee. Since it was essentially an agrarian-oriented party, there was some fear among state Democratic leaders that the Populists would woo the "plain folk" element and thereby make possible a Republican victory in the gubernatorial contest. But such apprehensions were ungrounded, for Buchanan, who ran as an Independent (with Populist support) after being denied the Democratic nomination, secured only 15 percent of the statewide vote. The Populist party was hurt by evidence, disclosed in the campaign, that its leaders were making deals with Republicans in various local contests. As a matter of fact, Populism as a distinct political party faded rapidly from the Tennessee scene, especially after the national Populist party decided to endorse the Democratic presidential candidate, William Jennings Bryan, in the 1896 election. Tennessee rural folk who had earlier moved away from the Democrats to join the Populists could now easily return to their traditional loyalties.

State Democrats had long been unhappy with the presence of black voters (estimated to be 80,000 in 1880), especially since they consistently cast Republican ballots. Although the poll tax as a requirement for voting was written into law shortly after ratification of the 1870 constitution, the law was repealed three years later. Consequently, blacks were voting without great handicap, and their votes were important. To curtail this influence the Democrats of the 1880s and 1890s attacked black political rights both in the larger cities, where blacks had gained a voice in local politics, and in the legislature. In Nashville, Memphis, and Chattanooga, partisan reformers focused their attention on trying to break up the old ward system of city politics in which blacks were active and which had enabled them to hold seats in city councils. Knoxville did not experience this reform effort, however, perhaps because of its smaller percentage of blacks and also the success of Democrats in local elections there. But in the other urban areas, the reformers' usual plan of attack was to amend the city charter to reduce greatly the number of wards and then to require all councilmen to run at large instead of by wards. The plan met with some success, but it was modest compared to the Democrats' achievements in restricting the black vote (as well as the poor-white vote) by legislative action.

The General Assembly, with Governor Bob Taylor's blessing, passed three laws directly related to voting rights in 1889, and then in special session the following year reactivated the poll tax. The first of the 1889 laws prescribed statewide voter registration in all towns and voting districts having five hundred voters or more. The second was a secret-ballot law, applicable in the four urban counties, which prohibited assistance to illiterates and thus served as a sort of educational qualification for voting (according to the 1890 figures, 52 percent of the black population was illiterate). Upon its passage, one advocate exclaimed: "It makes Tennessee Democratic . . . ." Also enacted was a law requiring separate ballot boxes for state elections when they were held simultaneously with national races—the effect of which was to prevent federal inspectors from checking the ballots in local elections. When the poll tax as a requirement for voting was added to the restrictive package, the access of blacks, as well as poor whites, to the ballot box was effectively limited. As a Nashville newspaper bluntly declared: "The Dortch law [secret ballot] and poll tax law solve the race problem in so far as the elections system is concerned." It was not an accident that, although twelve blacks served in the legislature in the 1880s, none was to serve again until the 1960s.

While the Jim Crow system was being implanted upon political rights of blacks in Tennessee and elsewhere in the South, lines of racial segregation and discrimination were being more tightly drawn. Steadfastly the state refused to support black education at a level comparable to the assistance given to white schools. No one, not even black leaders, challenged the segregated school system that had been dictated by the state constitution and by community mores. A few blacks served on local school boards in the 1880s, but that was the extent of their participation in governing the educational system of the state. With regard to public accommodations, the persistent problem on railroads was that some blacks paid first-class fares but got second-class accommodations in return. Segregation by race was not seriously questioned. In fact, the 1881 legislature, by decreeing that "separate but equal" facilities must be provided for blacks who paid first-class fares, officially sanctioned such discrimination. Ten years later Tennessee enacted a more comprehensive law along this line, in the same period that other Southern states were passing similar legislation, and in 1896 this "separate but equal" principle was given the authoritative blessing of the U.S. Supreme Court. Thus triumphed Jim Crow, which Neil R. McMillen has called "the most pertinacious bird in the southern skies."

At the same time that some reformers were busily trying to limit the opportunities and rights available to blacks in society, there were others who were joining the growing ranks of the prohibition crusade. In this post-Reconstruction period the advocates of temperance in drinking quickly became supporters of outright prohibition of alcohol—calling for a ban on its sale, manufacture, and consumption. By the late nineteenth century, in fact, the crusade had become so heated that the two terms, temperance and prohibition, were commonly used interchangeably. The prohibitionists achieved small but significant victories during this period, even though they would not see their efforts crowned with total success until the next century. Important steps toward their goal were taken in 1877, when the legislature agreed to prohibit the sale of liquor within four miles of any chartered school located in rural areas, and in 1899, when the Four Mile Law was extended to towns of 2,000 or fewer inhabitants.

The anti-liquor forces also succeeded in their push for a public referendum on a constitutional amendment to bring about statewide prohibition. The referendum was set for September 1887. Prohibitionists were now organized as the Tennessee Temperance Alliance, and they were aided considerably by the Woman's Christian Temperance Union and certain Protestant church groups, notably Baptists and Methodists. Opposing them were the anti-prohibition forces who had organized themselves as the State Protective Association. For almost eight months both sides waged a vigorous campaign, stimulating such widespread interest and controversy that in September approximately 263,000 Tennesseans went to the polls, which was 30,000 more than had voted in the "War of the Roses" gubernatorial race the year before. The amendment failed, the heaviest negative vote coming from Middle Tennessee, but the mounting strength of the anti-liquor movement was indicated by the large number of ballots cast in favor of the amendment: 45 percent of the voters asked for prohibition.

The prohibitionists also learned an important lesson during this period. In the 1880s and again in the 1890s when they fielded political candidates under the banner of the Prohibition party, they discovered the futility of trying to break the stranglehold of the two-party system. The best showing they made was in the 1890 governor's contest, when the Prohibition party candidate captured a mere 11,000 votes. In the twentieth century the prohibitionists would join the system rather than fight it.

The state's penal system was another object of reformers of the last two decades of the nineteenth century. The woefully inadequate prison facility in Nashville, which had been opened some sixty years earlier, was in dilapidated condition and seriously overcrowded. Despite the pleas of humanitarian crusaders for a new and much better state penitentiary, Tennessee, like a number of other states, answered prison problems by authorizing the convict-lease system. This was an arrangement whereby certain businesses were awarded state contracts that allowed them to use prison labor in exchange for specified sums of money paid to the state. The system met two very important needs. It relieved the over-crowded prison facilities and it brought in extra revenue for the state. Although recurring legislative investigations of the convict-lease system revealed that extremely poor treatment was being accorded state prisoners by various companies, political leaders generally chose to disregard the inhumane aspects and focused instead on the profits reaped

---

(*Above*): The new prison, the state's answer to the convict-lease system, featured an elaborate and ornate style. Courtesy Tennessee State Library and Archives. (*Below*): S.M. Patton fashioned this layout for the state penitentiary built in the late 1890s.

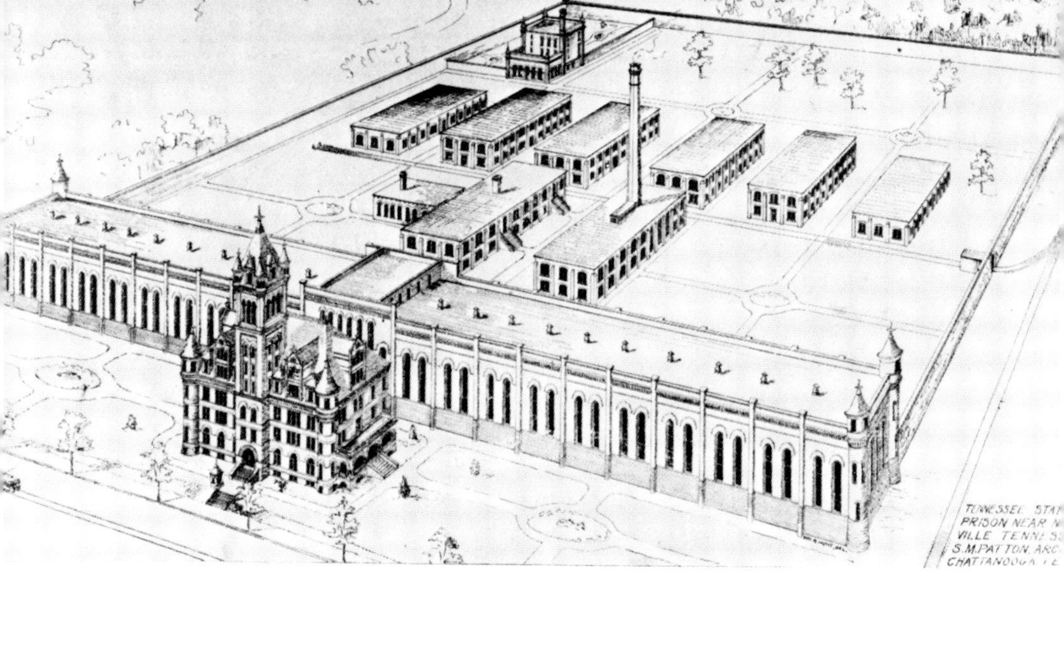
TENNESSEE STA
PRISON NEAR N
VILLE TENNES
S.M.PATTON, ARC
CHATTANOOGA

by state government ($771,000 in the twenty-year period, 1870–90). Furthermore, to break up the convict-lease system would have entailed the disruption of certain contractual arrangements—an undesirable precedent in the eyes of some leaders.

Several companies entered into leasing agreements with the state government, but the most important contract was signed in 1884, when the Tennessee Coal, Iron and Railroad Company became the exclusive hirer of state prisoners. Subsequently, the company was authorized to sublease some of the convicts, but in the main the Tennessee Coal Company held onto them and put them into its coal mines in Anderson, Roane, and Grundy counties. Overt violence erupted in 1891, when the regular miners could no longer tolerate the fact that prisoners, three-fourths of whom were blacks, took jobs away from free laborers. An additional grievance was that the company was using convicts to ward off possible unionization of the mines in East Tennessee. Beginning in July, coal miners forcibly released the convict laborers from the Anderson County mines. When Governor John Buchanan arrived to deal with the rebelling miners, he persuaded them to cease their violence, pledging in return to convene a special legislative session to consider terminating the convict-lease system. As promised, the General Assembly met in September, but it was unwilling to end the contract with the Tennessee Coal Company. Instead, in a display of independence or stubbornness, the legislature passed a law making it illegal to interfere with the convict-lease system! When news of this action reached East Tennessee, the incensed miners once more took the law into their own hands, releasing the convicts and sending them to Knoxville. An uneasy peace was eventually restored in early 1892 upon the arrival of General J. Keller Anderson, who quelled the miners' rebellion, at least temporarily, and returned the convicts to the mines.

Even more serious violence broke out in late summer, however, first in the mines of Grundy County and then in Anderson and Roane counties. Miners began burning down the convict stockades and freeing the prisoners, sending the convict laborers to the state prison at Nashville or to jails in Knoxville and other communities. Knoxvillians, who were ex-

---

(*Above*): Shown here are buildings on the grounds of the Centennial Exposition. (*Below*): A crowd awaits President McKinley at the Exposition in June 1897. Photographs from *Official History of the Tennessee Centennial Exposition.*

asperated with the continuing conflict in the adjacent coal-mining areas, began organizing volunteer units to go to Anderson County to put down the "wild, red-handed anarchists," as the Knoxville *Journal* dubbed the miners. But the volunteers made little headway, and the convict war was not brought under control until experienced state militia units marched into the area and made wholesale arrests of miners. About five hundred miners were arrested, but another twenty-seven were killed in skirmishes with the troops. When quiet eventually came to the coal fields, the Anderson County grand jury returned indictments against three hundred miners for conspiracy, for carrying arms, or for murder, but only a handful drew jail sentences or were even fined. The longest sentence, a seven-year prison term, was imposed upon a principal ringleader of the rebelling miners, who had been convicted of involuntary manslaughter.

Nevertheless, the convict war in the coal fields was largely responsible for achieving what the reformers had failed to accomplish: an end to the convict-lease system and the construction of a new state penitentiary. Weary of the conflict and attendant problems of keeping prison laborers in the mines, the General Assembly in the spring of 1893 passed a bill calling for abolition of the convict-lease arrangement and the erection of two new state prisons, one at Nashville and one in Morgan County at Petros. Two years later actual construction began at the Nashville site—which was the farm where Mark Cockrill had raised the finest wool in the world in antebellum times. The Nashville prison, still being used today, was not completed until 1898, but it was a modern facility for its time, comparing favorably with some of the best in the country. In Morgan County, the state purchased 9,000 acres of coal lands so that prisoners sent to the Brushy Mountain site could mine coal without competing with free laborers. Like the one in Nashville, the penitentiary at Brushy Mountain is still in use, more than eighty years after its opening. Convict leasing officially perished when the contract with the Tennessee Coal, Iron and Railroad Company expired at the end of 1895, making the state one of the first in the South to bring an end to this pernicious system.

The trend toward urbanization of Tennessee was launched during these last decades of the nineteenth century, as an increasing number of industries in the four major cities served as a magnet to draw new peo-

---

The Parthenon (*foreground*)—the lone survivor—the Commerce Building (*left*), and the Education Building (*right*) were Centennial Exposition structures. From *Official Views of United States Government Exhibits.*

ple, black and white, to urban life. The state as a whole had two million inhabitants in 1900—a figure double that of a half century earlier—but the population of Tennessee cities had increased by a slightly greater ratio (105 percent) in a mere ten years, from 1880 to 1890. In the census of 1900, more than 16 percent of all Tennesseans were shown to be living in the cities, a significant jump from the 4.2 percent recorded as urban dwellers in 1860. Memphis was the largest city as the old century ended and the new one began, boasting a population of 102,300, despite the yellow fever epidemics that caused it to lose population in the 1870s. Blacks, who turned increasingly to the cities in the post-Civil War period, represented almost half (50,000) of the Memphis residents in 1900. Nashville was the next largest city, with a total population of 80,800. Knoxville counted 35,600 people, and Chattanooga 30,100.

The century was drawing to a close when Tennesseans, as if to prove that the state had handled its ordeal of recovery and readjustment quite well, staged a mammoth centennial celebration in honor of the state's hundredth birthday. Nashville became the locale for the spectacle, partly because other Tennessee cities were content to sit back and permit the Middle Tennessee city to take the lead. To the embarrassment of some, the centennial exhibition failed to open in 1896, the anniversary year, but it was ready by the following May, and during the six months of its existence it drew 1.8 million visitors to the grounds of Centennial Park. Except to temperance crusaders and those government leaders expecting the state to prosper financially from the event, the exposition was a tremendous success. The setback, albeit slight, to the temperance movement occurred when the General Assembly circumvented probable controversy over selling beer and wine at the fair by declaring the park to be a separate, chartered city. The concession stands peddling the alcoholic beverages and other items did a brisk business, taking in nearly $125,000. Nevertheless, the fair as a whole barely broke even, receipts exceeding disbursements by a scant $39.00. Viewed from other angles, the exposition was a masterful achievement. It not only bequeathed the physical remains of the Parthenon and the park itself to future generations, but it also served the educational and socializing functions of bringing hundreds of thousands of people together to observe the latest developments in farming and industry. Most important, it stood as a dazzling symbol that closed the century on an optimistic note by saying that for most Tennesseans the thirty years since 1870 had been "a time to heal . . . and a time to build up." The state had passed its time of testing and was ready for the new ventures of the twentieth century.

4. Something Old, Something New, 1900–1970

As the twentieth century reached the three-quarters' mark, Tennessee still had not sent another Jackson, Polk, or Johnson to the White House, but the state obviously had retained its ability to capture national attention—whether the spotlighted event was praiseworthy or not. Ever a land of contrasts, Tennessee has continued this tradition in this current century. There was quiet, dignified Tennessean Cordell Hull, for instance, who after achieving acclaim as President Franklin Roosevelt's secretary of state won the Nobel Peace Prize for his work as "father" of the United Nations, and there was the tall, hand-shaking Estes Kefauver, avowed friend of the common man whose national popularity won him the Democratic nomination for Vice President. But also there was the evolution trial in Dayton, which indicted Tennessee as the "Monkey State," and four decades later there was the tragic assassination of Martin Luther King, Jr., in Memphis. Anderson County's brand new city of Oak Ridge was the site in the 1940s of remarkable and secret endeavors which resulted in the atomic bomb, while Clinton in the same county gained notoriety in the 1950s as the location of the state's first racial violence in conjunction with public school desegregation. In the depths of the Great Depression the Tennessee Valley Authority was established to rescue the region from undeniable economic backwardness, but TVA's legendary successes have in more recent times spawned mounting criticism from environmentalists and conservationists. From the most remote coves of the mountainous region of East Tennessee to the bustling metropolitan area of Memphis, some five hundred miles away, the state offers an enduring lesson in contrasts—something old, something new.

The major public issue facing Tennesseans as they moved into the new century, however, was not a new or contrasting one but instead a familiar question having deep roots in the previous century. It was the persistent moral and political crusade against alcohol. Marked by emotionalism and occasional violence, the controversy over prohibition in the first two decades reached an intensity seldom equalled before or since by a statewide issue. Not until 1920, when the Eighteenth Amendment made prohibition the law of the land, was the controversy—although continuing—subordinated to other concerns.

An 1877 law that appeared to be of limited application when first enacted became the basic instrument for drying up a large portion of the state by the early years of the twentieth century. Known as the "Four Mile Law" because it prohibited the sale of liquor within four miles of any rural school, the act was repeatedly amended so as to extend its provisions to Tennessee towns of certain specified populations. But a given town did not automatically become dry, for the law stipulated that a town wishing to forbid the sale of liquor had to surrender the town's charter and then reincorporate itself—a form of local option, one might argue. At any event, by 1903, when the Four Mile Law was amended again, alcohol sales were already forbidden in rural areas and in almost all towns of less than 2,000 residents. The 1903 amendment (the Adams Act) now opened the way to abolition of saloons in towns of 5,000 inhabitants or less. Prohibitionists greeted passage of this act with bell-ringing and thanksgiving services in many parts of Tennessee, and within a few months saloons were legal in only eleven out of the state's ninety-five counties.

The big cities were still legally wet, however. Even in 1907, when the Four Mile Law was extended to cities of 150,000, Knoxville was the only one of the four largest cities to qualify by reincorporating itself. Radical prohibitionists cried out for referendums to recharter Nashville and Chattanooga also. In Nashville, for instance, a local leader of the Woman's Christian Temperance Union urged fellow citizens to "throw off the yoke of bondage and join the procession of free cities redeemed from the curse of rum." But neither city responded with positive action. Thus, despite many successes, the prohibitionists had not dried up the state. Liquor still flowed freely from the wet cities into the dry sections of the state.

Meanwhile, temperance forces became increasingly involved in politics—to consolidate their gains and to push for total statewide prohibition. Led by the Tennessee Anti-Saloon League, they soon captured the Republican party and in 1910 and 1912 helped that party win the governor's chair. The prohibition question paved the way for these Republican victories by forcing a split in the dominant Democratic party. At the same time, the fight over alcohol contributed, at least in part, to the dramatic killing of prohibitionist Edward Ward Carmack. Carmack, a former U.S. senator, was a powerful political figure in Tennessee who had just completed an unsuccessful race for the Democratic nomination for governor in the 1908 primary. His opponent, the incumbent governor, Malcolm Patterson, won the nomination in one of the most hotly contested races in Tennessee history. Prohibition had been the central issue. In the immediate aftermath of the November general election, which Patterson won with little difficulty, Carmack, who was then editor of the Nashville *Tennessean,* directed extremely vitriolic editorials against the Patterson organization and in particular against Duncan B. Cooper, an adviser to the governor. Cooper sent a warning to the editor that Nashville could not hold both of them, but Carmack persisted in his journalistic attacks and also armed himself with a pistol. In the afternoon following the appearance of another Carmack editorial deriding Cooper, the two antagonists, along with Cooper's son, met on a downtown Nashville street. It was apparently a chance meeting, but a gun battle ensued, and Carmack was killed. He became an instant martyr for the prohibition forces.

The Democratic party, already torn by the inflamed emotions of the 1908 elections, was now hopelessly divided, which permitted an alliance of Republicans and prohibition Democrats to gain control of both houses of the General Assembly. In 1909, the alliance pushed through a bill (the Holladay Act) that outlawed the sale of liquor within four miles of any school and did not require cities to recharter—which had the effect of providing for prohibition in all parts of the state. Further, in an effort to dry up local sources of liquor, the prohibition-minded legislature approved a bill to halt the manufacture of alcohol in the state.

Tennessee presumably was now a state that embraced prohibition almost totally, but in fact it did not. The interstate shipment of alcohol continued, and the refusal of the state's major cities to comply with the anti-liquor laws made a mockery of the legislative successes of the prohibition forces. A liquor newspaper reported in 1910 that more liquor was being sold in Tennessee than ever before. That was the year that the Republicans, pointing to the failure of the Democrats to enforce the prohibition laws, elected a governor of their own party: Ben W. Hooper, an East Tennessee attorney and staunch prohibitionist. Although Hooper was re-elected two years later, the Republican reign was over. The Democrats won majorities in both houses of the legislature that same year and thereafter, shrewdly seizing upon statewide prohibition as their own goal, returned to full power with Democratic Governor Thomas Rye, elected in 1914.

From Rye's election until 1920 when the Eighteenth Amendment put prohibition on a nationwide basis, the experience in Tennessee demonstrated the extreme difficulty, if not impossibility, of completely shutting off the flow of liquor to those who wanted it. During Rye's two terms as governor, for instance, the General Assembly enacted rigorous legislation designed to enforce the state's prohibition laws. One was the Ouster Law (authorizing the removal of government officials for neglect of duties, such as failing to uphold prohibition measures), which succeeded in displacing Nashville Mayor Hilary Howse and in forcing the resignation of Memphis Mayor Edward H. Crump, both loyal Democrats but also avowed foes of prohibition. Another new law made it illegal to receive or possess liquor delivered by carrier, but even these stringent laws were not totally effective. In the ensuing years, until national prohibition was repealed in 1933, Tennessee continued to struggle with most of the same problems that had been encountered in the state prior to 1920—corrupt or uninterested public officials and, most of all, a lack of total commitment by the citizenry to the prohibition cause. The fight against alcohol persists, of course, although largely on the local level. Opposing forces in a local option referendum often reach peaks of emotion and bitterness that are reminiscent of earlier times. It is also true that the illicit liquor trade, in its various forms, continues to find profitable business in those communities and counties that have voted to close the door to legal liquor.

Tennessee's action in ratifying the Eighteenth Amendment in 1919 had been expected by national observers. After all, the state was already legally dry. But when the woman's suffrage amendment—the Nineteenth—came up for a vote in Tennessee the following year, the outcome was highly uncertain. By the summer of 1920, thirty-five states had chosen to give women the right to vote and ratification by only one more state was needed. But at least eight Southern states had already turned down the proposition. How would Tennessee—a Border state looking to the North in some matters but tenaciously allied to the South in others—react to this question?

The state's history of dealing with woman's suffrage had been somewhat spotty. As with prohibition, the crusade had its beginnings in the late nineteenth century. Following the 1895 visits to Tennessee of the national suffrage leaders Susan B. Anthony and Carrie Chapman Catt, state leaders generated enough enthusiasm to form a Tennessee Equal Rights Association. But the suffrage excitement soon waned, and it was late 1906 before new life was breathed into the feminist campaign with the establishment of the Tennessee Equal Suffrage Association. Even from that time on, however, the approach of the woman's suffrage proponents was cautious and conservative. Giving little evidence of the militancy that characterized the movement in a few other states, they nevertheless had their highly vocal detractors. From time to time Tennessee's rural legislators warned that woman's suffrage would lead to urban domination of politics. Liquor interests, apparently believing that many women favored prohibition, generally opposed the suffrage movement, and certain fundamentalist church groups likewise spoke out against the feminists. Opposition also came from other women, who in 1916 organized a Tennessee chapter of the National Association Opposed to Woman Suffrage. Oddly enough, it was not until the state suffrage leaders themselves split into two rival groups—arguing over which city would host the national convention of the woman's suffrage association coming to Tennessee in 1914—that the state movement began to make legislative progress. A near victory was achieved in 1915 when the General Assembly approved a state constitutional amendment granting voting rights to women, but the necessary approval by a subsequent legislative session failed to materialize. Then in 1919 a bill was passed (it had been rejected two years earlier) that allowed women to vote in municipal and presidential elections—but not, however, in congressional, legislative, gubernatorial, and county contests.

Thus, as the time approached for convening of the special session of the legislature, called for August 1920 to consider ratification of the Nineteenth Amendment, tension mounted. Leaders of rival groups poured into Nashville, virtually taking over the two major hotels. When the session opened, Governor Albert H. Roberts urged passage of the amendment, and the state senate ratified it with no difficulty. But the prediction of a close vote was borne out by action of the lower house. A motion to table ratification barely failed, yielding a 48 to 48 vote and forcing the chamber to vote directly on ratification. The Nineteenth Amendment finally cleared the house by the slim margin of a 50 to 46 vote—only after Harry Burn, a Republican legislator from East Tennessee, switched sides to favor ratification and was joined by the house speaker, Seth Walker, who also changed his vote. Disgruntled legislators complained that the ratification had not been legally carried out, but it became a moot argument when state officials forwarded word of ratification to a generally jubilant nation.

A few months later the newly enfranchised women made their presence felt at the ballot box when they participated in the presidential and

SPECIAL SESSION
SUFFRAGE
ANTI-SUFFRAGE
TENNESSEE LEGISLATURE

ANTI-RATIFICATION
HEADQUARTERS
AND
EXHIBITION
FORREST VETERAN SCOUTS

state elections. In the national contest Tennessee voted for Republican Warren G. Harding—the first time the state had gone for a Republican presidential candidate since 1868. In the governor's race the state chose Republican Alfred A. Taylor (the last Republican gubernatorial victory for half a century). In both elections female voters seemed to have been decisively Republican in their preferences. Nowhere was this more apparent than in East Tennessee, which not only experienced a tremendous increase in the number of voters, but also gave such heavy margins to the Republican contenders that the traditional Democratic leanings of Middle and West Tennessee could not offset them. Shortly thereafter, however, Democrats regained control of state politics and held on to it for the remainder of the decade.

As evidenced by the Carmack killing, Tennesseans did not resolve their conflicts solely at the ballot box during the first twenty years of the century. In West Tennessee, for instance, violence erupted in 1908 over a purely local matter—the ownership of Reelfoot Lake. Then in 1917–18, nearly 80,000 Tennesseans joined the nation's World War I expeditionary forces to settle a conflict on foreign soil.

The tranquil beauty of Reelfoot Lake, in the extreme northwest corner of the state, belies the controversy that surrounded it in earlier days. A hunting and fishing mecca and Tennessee's major natural lake, it was formed when the spectacular New Madrid earthquake of 1811–12 dammed up the Reelfoot River. A serious conflict over the lake arose as early as the 1890s when James C. Harris began buying up land in the area and parts of the lake itself, thereby curtailing access to it by local fishermen and hunters who used it commercially. Although an attempt was made to block Harris's purchases by court action, the state supreme court eventually ruled in 1902 that the lake was not navigable and therefore, according to state law, it could be privately owned. After Harris's death, when his son and others formed a land company to complete the

---

(*Above*): This cartoon typifies those of 1920 when both suffrage and anti-suffrage forces wooed the legislature. (*Below*): Anti-suffrage leaders shown at their Hermitage Hotel headquarters are Mrs. James A. Pinckard (*left*), president general of the Southern Women's League, and Josephine Pearson (*right*), president of the Tennessee chapter. A former Confederate soldier, William A.P. Crutcher (*center*), symbolizes earlier states rights beliefs. Illustrations courtesy Tennessee State Library and Archives.

acquisition of the lake area, various individuals again sought relief in the courts, but without success.

Following this failure, the protesters resorted to force and intimidation in an effort to regain use of the lake area. Forming a group that came to be known as "night riders," they instilled fear in area residents and directed national attention to Tennessee by their abusive tactics. Even those not directly involved in the conflict over the lake were attacked. For example, a Lake County official, who reportedly said that blacks were better than night riders, was mercilessly beaten by a dozen night riders and subsequently died as a result of the assault. But it was in October 1908 that the violence reached a climax when two land company lawyers were kidnapped. One of them, Quentin Rankin, was hanged and shot, but the other miraculously escaped. The reaction was immediate. Governor Patterson called out the state militia, and Pinkerton detectives hired by the land company aided in rounding up all possible suspects in the Rankin case. Newspapers, several of them from other states, sent "war correspondents" to the scene to report on the arrest and trial of the night riders.

In the courts, the eight night riders who were indicted managed to escape punishment altogether. Although six of them were found guilty of first-degree murder and the other two were convicted of second-degree murder, the state supreme court reversed the verdicts because of procedural errors. All eight were thus set free. The state of Tennessee, however, was more successful in a related case. Fearing additional unrest, the state declared that the lake should be publicly owned and attempted to reach an agreement with the land company. Failing in these efforts, the state then brought suit in a case heard by the supreme court in 1913. This time, the court reversed its earlier opinion and ruled that the lake was indeed navigable and consequently not eligible for private ownership. Eventually, in 1925, a state game and fish preserve was established at Reelfoot Lake.

Compared with the immediacy of the violence at Reelfoot Lake, the battles and casualties of World War I, despite their greater significance, seemed far away to the state at large. To those directly affected, of course, this war to stop the military machine of the German Kaiser and

---

Sgt. Alvin C. York poses shortly after the end of World War I wearing his Congressional Medal of Honor and the French Croix de Guerre. Courtesy Tennessee State Museum.

to avenge the sinking of U.S. ships was intensely real and in some cases a personal tragedy. Tennessee gave to the nation and the world a hero of giant proportions: Sergeant Alvin C. York, who during the battle of Argonne Forest single-handedly took on the German army. His exploits, killing twenty enemy soldiers and capturing more than a hundred others, won him overnight international acclaim. He was awarded the Congressional Medal of Honor and the State of Tennessee gave him a farm in his home county of Fentress. And fifty years later, a statue of York was placed on the state capitol grounds. During the brief period of American involvement in World War I, Tennessee had no military training camps, but the colleges helped to train officers through the Reserve Officer Training Corps programs. In this state, as was true throughout the nation, persons of German ancestry were suspect, the teaching of the German language was forbidden in the schools, and even musical works by German composers could not be played. Even though the war disrupted the routine of everyday life to some extent and brought the loss of lives to some Tennessee homes, most Tennesseans did not feel the direct impact of the war to the degree that they would in later global conflicts.

But whether Tennessee residents knew it or not, the First World War did have an influence on the state's economy. The European demand for agricultural products, for instance, boosted farm prices considerably during the period from about 1914 until the conclusion of the war. But then, perhaps as a harbinger of the Great Depression of the 1930s, the prices of farm products plummeted drastically in a recession which followed the wartime inflation. Similarly, manufacturing increased dramatically in response to wartime needs and then suffered a post-war recession. Unlike agriculture, however, which never again became the dominant sector of the state's economy, manufacturing seemed to recover satisfactorily in a few years, and by 1930 the value of its products exceeded that of farm products by a margin of more than two to one. Tennessee was emerging as an industrial state, a transformation that would become increasingly evident in succeeding decades.

After the war, when the Democratic party once again took charge of state politics, Tennesseans elected Austin Peay, a remarkable politician who was to become one of the state's outstanding governors. He defeated the incumbent Republican Alf Taylor in 1922 and then went on to win handily in 1924 and 1926, making him the first governor in sixty years to win three consecutive terms. Initially riding the wave of business progressivism in the post-war period, Peay got the enthusiastic backing of business and urban interests who wanted efficiency and economy in state government. But Peay's aggressive programs soon earned him the enmity of these original supporters; they eventually tagged him with the "Robin Hood" label, charging that his policies were robbing the wealthier counties and giving to the poorer ones. Increasingly, Peay was compelled to turn to the small town and rural interests to win support for his brand of post-war reforms. That they backed him was evident in the 1926 election, when Peay carried all three sections of the state—a fitting reward for his careful cultivation of Republican East Tennessee. Peay's victory in that year was the beginning of a forty-year period during which the Republicans did not command the strength to compete seriously in the races for governor. From that point on, the important political battles were waged in the Democratic party primaries rather than in the general elections. This trend was of course given a semblance of permanence in the 1930s by the Great Depression, which so many voters throughout the nation seemed to blame on the Republicans.

Not only did Peay prove himself a consummate politician, but he also demonstrated notable abilities as an administrator and leader of state government. He first directed his energies and talents to the task of reorganizing government, a need impressed upon him by his early business supporters. With the cooperation of the General Assembly, the governor eliminated more than sixty bureaus, commissions, and boards (largely the creation of irresponsible legislators) and established instead eight departments, all directly answerable to the governor. Next, noting that the state could claim no more than 250 miles of paved roads, Peay launched a highway construction program, financed by a new tax on gasoline, that within five or six years had laced Tennessee with thousands of miles of hard-surfaced state highways. Very early in his administration, Peay pleased many voters, especially the rural, agricultural ones, by pushing through a reduction in the state property tax. To offset the loss of revenue, a 3 percent excise tax was imposed on corporate net profits.

Peay's progressive program even extended to environmental and conservation concerns. It was through his efforts, for example, that Reelfoot Lake became a state game and fish preserve. In addition to making sure that new highways were built in East Tennessee, the Democratic governor continued his courtship of that Republican region by supporting the movement for a national park in the Great Smoky Mountains. Today's most popular national park, this area of lush vegetation and great scenic beauty was also the first national park to be acquired from private owners and given by the people of a region to the federal government. The first step toward land acquisition for the proposed park was made in 1925 when the state purchased the Little River tract. Two years later Governor Peay enthusiastically endorsed the issuance of $1.5 million of state bonds for the purchase of additional lands. These actions, plus purchases made by North Carolina, and much ground work and fund raising (in which even school children participated) by Knoxville-area residents, eventually attracted $5 million from the Rockefeller family in 1928 and led to the establishment of the Great Smoky Mountains National Park by Congress in the 1930s. In September 1940 thousands of citizens gathered at Newfound Gap to take part in the park's dedication ceremonies, led by President Franklin Roosevelt.

Despite the significance of Governor Peay's other accomplishments, his sponsorship of the Education Act of 1925 stands out as one of the major milestones in the history of Tennessee public education. Education still had a long way to go in the state when Peay took office, even though tremendous progress had been made in the preceding twenty years. At the beginning of the century, the state's education system was deplorable, as was true in many Southern states. For example, there were no state-supported high schools in Tennessee, less than half of the state's eligible children actually attended school, teachers' salaries were barely measurable, and there was only one state university, the University of Tennessee—which was a state school in name only, having received no funds at all from the state government. But beginning in 1903 with Governor James B. Frazier's appointment of Seymour Mynders as state superintendent of public instruction, the first professionally trained educator to hold that post, the cause of education had come to life. Pushing the issue to public attention were interested governors and legislators, an increasingly active "school lobby," and professional educators such as Mynders. Among these leading educators was Philander P. Claxton, who was appointed U.S. commissioner of education during this period. Claxton had previously directed the Summer School of the South at the University of Tennessee, a short-term training school for teachers that became nationally famous during its brief heyday.

Among the advances achieved by these education forces were the establishment of county high schools, improvement in the training of

---

(*Above*): During his 1926 campaign, Governor Austin Peay spoke before a July 4 crowd near Tiptonville. Courtesy Nashville *Tennessean*. (*Below*): One-room schools were a feature of public education in the early 1900s. Courtesy TVA.

GOV. AUSTIN PEAY
GOVERNOR

teachers, creation of school libraries, and the initiation of school consolidation and pupil transportation. During Governor Patterson's administration, the legislature decreed that the county should become the school district—an important reform that dramatically reduced the then-existing 3,300 separate school districts down to ninety-five. Also during the Patterson years, two-year training institutions for teachers (called normal schools in those days) were established at Johnson City, Murfreesboro, and Memphis; and an agricultural-industrial institute for blacks (now Tennessee State University) was built in Nashville. In addition, the University of Tennessee was given regular financial support by the state and made an integral part of the state school system. Critical to such advances, of course, was financing. A major gain was recorded in 1909 when the General Assembly provided that 25 percent of the state's gross revenue should go to support the public schools, and additional provisions for funding education were enacted by subsequent legislatures.

Peay's administration and the General Assembly built on this base to carry education another major step forward. The governor's reorganization of state government elevated the status of education by making it one of the eight newly-established departments. And the General Education Law of 1925 crowned his efforts by providing state funding to make possible an eight-month school term in all counties and by supplementing teachers' salaries. Moreover, the licensing of teachers was standardized and the state normal schools were converted into four-year teachers' colleges. And two years later the governor prodded the legislature into appropriating even more funds for state education. Insofar as state financing of schools is concerned, a simple comparison indicates the strides made: in 1900 the state gave only about $130,000 to public schools, whereas in 1925 it contributed approximately $3.2 million. One very important byproduct of the total achievements of Peay during his three terms as governor was an amassing of more power in the chief executive's office—a concentration that in time proved to be a two-edged sword.

It was also during Peay's administration that Tennesseans provided another example of their controversial nature. The same 1925 legislature that was to promote education so effectively brought notoriety to the state by taking what many observers, especially those in other states, called a backward step. The General Assembly passed the Butler bill, which outlawed the teaching of evolution in the public schools. Governor Peay, after delaying action for several days, finally signed the measure, apparently fearing that a veto would jeopardize passage of his education bill. The author of the anti-evolution bill, as well as a vast number of other Tennesseans of fundamentalist faiths that adhered to a narrow interpretation of the Bible, believed the law necessary to combat what they felt were increasing attacks on Christianity. Charles Darwin's theory of evolution was particularly offensive to them because it conflicted directly with the story of creation recorded in the Book of Genesis.

Almost immediately after the Butler bill was signed, John Thomas Scopes, a young biology teacher at Dayton, was arrested and indicted for violation of the new law. The arrest was admittedly a contrived situation, perhaps to test the anti-evolution law but more likely, it was said, to bring publicity and visitors to Dayton. But the somewhat jocular spirit which prevailed in the early stages of the episode evaporated in the intense heat of courtroom arguments. Local luminaries took a back seat to William Jennings Bryan, high priest of religious fundamentalism, who arrived in Dayton to do battle for the anti-evolution crusade; and to Clarence Darrow, irreverent apostle of free-thinking and evolution. Meanwhile the presiding judge, John T. Raulston, enjoyed himself immensely, especially when posing for pictures or making statements over the radio.

For eight sweltering days in July the Scopes trial dragged on, with one of the greatest spectacles being Darrow's incisive cross-examination of Bryan. Most major newspapers of the nation reported the proceedings. The trial ended with Darrow pleading for a conviction of Scopes so that the matter could be appealed to a higher court. The jury complied, and Judge Raulston levied a $100 fine against Scopes. About eighteen months later the state supreme court upheld the validity of the Butler Law but on technical grounds dismissed the fine imposed upon Scopes.

Although never again enforced, the Butler Law remained on the statute books until its repeal in 1967, and Tennessee continued to be labelled the "Monkey State." At the time of its initial passage, the law was a symbol of the collective fears of those who found their traditional beliefs and customs challenged by the onslaught of urbanism, industrialism, and the greater mobility of their society. But as the years went by, the Butler Law increasingly became a mere monument to past anxieties.

Also expressing concern about the changes in society and culture was a group of students and faculty at Vanderbilt University in the 1920s who earned a lasting place in the history of Southern literature. Known as the Fugitives (because of their journal, *The Fugitive*), these poets and essayists wrote of the virtues of creativity and individualism and decried crass materialism so apparent on every hand in the decade. They exerted a great influence upon the Southern literary renaissance that continues even today. Closely allied with this group was a second body of scholars at Vanderbilt, the Agrarians, who emerged near the end of the decade. In fact, at least four of the Agrarians had also been members of the Fugitive group. Of the twelve Agrarians who published *I'll Take My Stand* (1930), their chief manifesto, most were interested in literature, but there were also two historians and a psychologist in the group. As their name suggests, these writers extolled the rural, agrarian way of life. They warned that industrialization and urbanization could erode the human soul, and they longed nostalgically for the past when the slower-paced agrarian life granted time for contemplation of nobler things. As self-appointed defenders of the South, the Agrarians were particularly concerned about the changes being wrought by the engines of progress. The South, they argued, should never succumb to imitating the vices of the industrial Northeast. Not all of the Agrarians closed their eyes to the future, however, for several urged the need to adjust to change—although not at the price of losing one's soul. Today's students encountering the Agrarians' writings for the first time, fifty years after the original publication date, often find them to be closely akin to current concerns about environmental dangers resulting from giant industrial activity and overcrowded cities.

Other Tennesseans, many more than were represented by the Agrarians, also looked to the past—but in somewhat different ways. In the 1920s, country music blossomed and flourished in Tennessee as it had never done before. The music's root sources—ballads, folk songs, and hymns—had of course been a part of the state's culture for generations, but the radio and recording studios spawned by technological advances in the post-World War I years gave widespread vitality to this Tennessee music. In the 1920s while George Pullen Jackson, a leading Tennessee folklorist, collected white spirituals, Sterchi Brothers Furniture Store in Knoxville helped agents of the Aeolian-Vocalion Record Company identify and locate country music performers throughout the state. Tennessee proved to be very fertile soil, with Uncle Dave Macon and Sam McGee being only two of the most popular singers and players who recorded during this decade. Meanwhile in Lawrenceburg, James D. Vaughan founded his famous singing school, which soon led to the publication of songbooks, records, and magazines. In time Vaughan would become one of the leading developers and promoters of gospel music throughout the nation. But Tennessee's reputation as a haven for banjos, guitars, fiddles, and nostalgic ballads was to be established primarily through the popularity of the Grand Ole Opry, which began broadcasting in late 1925. Fourteen years later, the NBC network started carrying a portion of the Opry on Saturday night, and Hollywood produced a movie, "The Grand Ole Opry," with Roy Acuff in a leading role. Thus to the eyes and ears of the nation, Tennessee country music had arrived. But along the way, in the process of commercialization, much of the original style and message of such music had been altered. Cecil Sharp, who first began collecting mountain folk songs in Tennessee in 1916, would have been surprised and perhaps displeased at the changes that had taken place.

Although a black harmonica player, Deford Bailey, was one of the most popular solo performers on the Opry in the 1920s, black Tennesseans generally remained on the periphery of the state's life in the first thirty years of the century. Concern over racial segregation on public transportation, evident in the late nineteenth century, continued into the twentieth when the 1905 General Assembly enacted a segregation law which applied to the seating on streetcars in all cities. Although blacks organized boycotts of streetcars across Tennessee, they enjoyed success, albeit modest, only in Nashville. Eventually black leadership in the capital city decided to establish a black-owned streetcar company, but the Union Transportation Company led a precarious existence until midsummer of 1906 when it finally ceased operations. The black protest having failed, segregated seating on streetcars became the entrenched practice throughout the state.

In matters of education and politics black Tennesseans scored few gains. Despite the recognizable advances made in public education, there was little improvement for blacks. It took the money and work of four out-of-state philanthropic organizations to help narrow the gap between educational opportunities for blacks and whites in Tennessee. In the political realm blacks saw themselves being excluded more and more from their traditional Republican home. Only in Memphis, thanks to the remarkable leadership of Robert R. Church, Jr., did blacks continue their strong identity and role within the Republican party. Black Tennesseans did unite in the 1920s, however, to fight against the resurgence of the Ku Klux Klan, which sought to run candidates for municipal offices in both Memphis and Chattanooga. In the elections held in 1923 in those two cities the black electorate was instrumental in defeating nearly all of the Klan candidates.

On the economic front, blacks experienced mixed results. The demands of the war-time economy in the decade, 1910–20, led to a general improvement in prosperity for black laborers in the cities and also black farmers. Despite the latter development, the black exodus from the farms to the cities continued unabated in the first twenty years of the century—as seen in the industrial cities of East Tennessee which experienced a 54 percent increase in their black population. Other statistics indicate the statewide story: whereas 30 percent of the state's black residents was urban in 1900, that figure rose to slightly over 50 percent in 1930. Four black-owned banks and one black insurance company were established in Tennessee prior to 1930—all helped by improving levels of the economy during the war years. But the unregulated and unsound banking practices, so characteristic of the nation in this era, took a heavy toll in Tennessee in the 1920s—fifty-nine banks went bankrupt, including three of the four black-owned banks. The Universal Life Insurance Company, founded in Memphis, continued to prosper, however, so that by 1930 it was one of the eight largest black insurance companies in the nation.

The year 1919 was a time of racial turmoil in a number of cities scattered throughout the United States, and Tennessee did not escape. Knoxville, a city of small black population and seemingly harmonious race relations, was the scene of a race riot in the late summer, sparked by the arrest of a black man for the alleged murder of a white woman. The violence, involving rioting by both races, was rooted in white uneasiness over black mobility and concentration in the cities, the whites apparently fearing challenges to the existing caste system. The state was shocked by the disruptions in Knoxville, some people declaring that if such problems could erupt there, then no place was immune from the possibility of racial conflict. But in actuality, there was little overt racial strife prior to 1930. Later decades would bring plenty, however.

For all Tennesseans, black and white, the Great Depression of the 1930s and World War II of the succeeding decade changed their world in diverse and profound ways. The urban areas bore much of the brunt of the economic depression when thousands were thrown out of work overnight. The sounds of banks closing their doors for the last time, of hammers nailing shut small businesses, and of hushed voices of people in soup lines discussing their plight with fellow sufferers—these were the new sounds of urban life as the reputed glamour and excitement of the twenties quickly vanished. The psychological repercussions of these experiences defy quantification, but they were real nevertheless. One young Chattanooga worker captured some of the emotional distress in a poignant recollection: "I remember lying in bed one night and thinking. All at once I realized something. We were poor. Lord! It was weeks before I could get over that. I was ashamed to look at anybody and to talk to them. I thought everybody was saying to themselves, 'This Douglas boy is poor.'" A similar realization must have crowded in upon thousands who formerly had been making a respectable living only to find themselves suddenly out of work and out in the streets.

Likewise the war years etched themselves upon the emotions and lives of the people. After all, nearly 10 percent of the state's population served in the armed forces. Not only were they uprooted from their jobs and schooling, but thousands of them became casualties of the prolonged war against Germany and Japan. For those who waited anxiously at home, the war meant food and gasoline rationing, scrap iron drives, and victory gardens. The celebrations in Tennessee towns over the American victories in Europe and Japan in 1945 saw a great outpouring of gratitude and joy that the long night of war was over. But those who thought that things would now return to normal were mistaken, for the world, the nation, and the state had all been transformed by both the war's experiences and the Great Depression. Returning veterans were among the first to recognize this new reality.

The state's farmers who had already been experiencing problems in the 1920s were hit hard by the national depression. But they were rescued from possible total ruin by the various New Deal programs enacted and implemented by the federal government in the 1930s. The Agricultural Adjustment Act, designed to raise farm prices to parity, had a tremendously beneficial impact upon Tennessee farmers during its three years of existence. The same was true of the Commodity Credit Corporation and the Rural Electrification Administration as they brought relief and aid to the agricultural sector. Certainly the Tennessee Valley Authority, established in 1933, made important progress in teaching better and more scientific methods of agriculture to the region's farmers. But although some recovery was evident by the end of the decade, it took the extraordinary demands of a wartime economy in the 1940s to lift agriculture to new prosperity.

Throughout most of the 1930–70 period a declining number of farms, decreasing farm acreage, and a shrinking farm population were facts of life in Tennessee—a trend that actually had its beginnings in the 1920s. The exception to this general pattern occurred in the 1930s when there were increases, not decreases, in farm population, number of farms, and acreage; this was explained partly by the successes of the New Deal

1831
McCORMICK
REAPER
CENTENNIAL
1931
CARDUI

programs in making farm life more bearable. Moreover, faced with a severe economic depression many persons perhaps reasoned that it was better to take one's chance out on the farm where at least a few crops could be grown to help put food on the table. Ironically, once the agricultural economy began improving in the early 1940s, as a consequence of the demands and needs of the war years, people began leaving the farms again for the cities, a trend that continued through 1970. In 1930 the farm population was 1.2 million, but by 1970 it had shrunk to only 317,000. The 245,000 farms in 1930 had been cut in half by 1970, and the 18 million acres under cultivation in 1930 had dropped to 15 million by 1970. To offset these losses, there was a tremendous growth in farm productivity, for without exception the yield per acre for the major crops jumped markedly in the forty years after 1930. Chiefly responsible for these achievements were modern fertilizing techniques, better farming practices, improved strains of seeds, and the mechanization of the farms. With the latter came the disappearance of mules and horses on Tennessee farms. The advent of tractors (only about 12,000 in 1940 but nearly 100,000 by 1960) brought a new day to the agricultural scene.

The Tennessee Valley Authority, born to bring economic uplift to farmers and nonfarmers alike, was established in direct response to the Great Depression, and TVA, like the state as a whole, was also challenged and changed by World War II. Years ago John Gunther, with perhaps only slight exaggeration, wrote, "the TVA idea is the greatest single American invention of this century." Tennessee farmers, as well as industrialists, have echoed such sentiments repeatedly across the years. The agency has touched the lives of all Tennessee residents in three basic areas: production of electricity, river development and flood control, and agricultural improvements. In the wake of TVA's activities and programs have come phenomenal changes in the region. As David Lilienthal, one of the original TVA directors, observed: "This is an entirely different region from what it once was. You can see the change almost everywhere you go. . . . And marching toward every point on the horizon you can see the steel crisscross of electric transmission towers, a

---

(*Above*): At a country store, the focal point of rural communities, an interviewer for the newly-created TVA talks to prospective workers. (*Below*): The advent of mechanical equipment on Tennessee farms in post-World War II days greatly improved farming methods. Photographs courtesy TVA.

twentieth-century tower standing in a cove beside an eighteenth-century mountain cabin, a symbol and a summary of change."

But TVA was not able to bring about such a transformation without problems or controversy. It is sometimes easy to forget that during its first six years the agency spent a great deal of time in preparing legal briefs and presenting them in various federal courts. In that period there were fifty-seven lawsuits and twenty-six injunctions to stop TVA from developing hydroelectric capacities and from distributing electricity once the dams were built. Luckily for TVA and its regional program, it won all of the court challenges. Construction of Norris Dam, the first in the system, brought bitterness and hostility from those people in East Tennessee who were removed from their homes and relocated elsewhere. Also a personality and philosophical conflict flared up within TVA's board of directors, with the eventual result that in 1938 President Roosevelt removed Arthur Morgan, the board chairman.

Once the initial difficulties were overcome, new ones arose. The decision to build the Douglas Dam on the French Broad River, for example, stirred a great deal of resentment, especially from prominent families who stood to lose valuable farm land. They were joined in opposition by Senator Kenneth McKellar of Tennessee, a man increasingly disenchanted with TVA because of its refusal to yield to his pressure for appointments for his friends. But the outbreak of World War II and the sudden new demands for electricity enabled TVA to win the battle over Douglas Dam. In the 1950s the agency faced an unexpected threat when President Eisenhower appointed General Herbert Vogel to be chairman of TVA's board, with the understanding that Vogel would help dismantle the agency. But instead, Vogel became a convert to TVA's programs and worked to promote them. Apprehensive about its future, TVA decided to seek congressional approval to become self-financing by issuing revenue bonds for construction projects. Permission was given in 1959 and TVA emerged in a stronger position than ever—ready for future accomplishments and controversies.

In the years since the Great Depression, TVA's power production plans

---

(*Above*): President and Mrs. Roosevelt visit the Norris Dam site in 1934. Seated next to them is Arthur E. Morgan, first chairman of the TVA Board of Directors. (*Below*): The large poster behind the speaker's platform at the Douglas Dam dedication testified to TVA's war effort. Photographs courtesy TVA.

Out of water power
comes air power
THESE TVA DAMS
ARE NEEDED FOR
VICTORY
RPM
EMERGENCY SIREN
FOR
FIRE ONLY!
Remove Jacket Before Using

have been altered drastically. Originally the agency intended to produce only hydroelectric power, but World War II changed that. Steam-generated electricity was, of necessity, added during the war years to meet the unprecedented power demands in the region. Thus by 1970, hydroelectric power accounted for only 20 percent of TVA's output, whereas steam plants produced 80 percent. This dramatic shift has made the agency the largest coal consumer in the entire nation, which, in turn, has encouraged strip mining in the region. Despite the transformation in power production, TVA has blessed the region with cheap electric rates. Steadily rising rates have somewhat weakened the agency's support by the public, however, although the development and expansion of nuclear plants may help TVA to restrain these increases in the future.

Besides providing abundant electricity of relatively low cost, TVA has boosted the state's economy in manifold other ways. Hundreds of thousands of Tennesseans have been employed by the agency during its more than forty years of existence. TVA's flood control program has averted flood damage that would have cost millions of dollars. The agency's development of man-made lakes has been a boon to recreational and tourist activities in the state. Moreover, in its early days TVA established demonstration parks and subsequently gave them to the state. This generosity launched the development of Tennessee's excellent state parks system, which prior to the arrival of TVA was nonexistent. It may be fairly claimed that no other governmental agency, state or federal, has been more involved in the lives of Tennesseans than TVA, bringing improvements, economic uplift, and enduring change.

From its beginnings to the present day, TVA has had a beneficial impact upon Tennessee manufacturing, but it has had to share this honor, oddly enough, with a war. The state's industries were severely hurt by the depression in the thirties, causing declines in both the number of manufacturing establishments and the value of their products, but because of the demands of World War II the industrial sector recovered rapidly in the 1940s and thereafter enjoyed unprecedented growth and development. To help the American fighting man in Europe and the Pa-

---

(*Above*): The steel transmission towers shown here are tangible symbols of regional modernization brought about by TVA. (*Below*): Unprecedented demands for electricity forced TVA into generating steam rather than hydroelectric power. The Bull Run Steam Plant, near Oak Ridge, began operation in the 1960s. Photographs courtesy TVA.

cific, Tennessee industries in the early 1940s busily produced clothing, food, munitions, arms, and ships, while employing 200,000 men and women for the war effort. The companies thus involved received war contracts amounting to a total of $1.2 billion. The war years consequently resulted in a substantial boost in the number of industrial plants and employees and also in the emergence of the chemical industry as the state's leading manufacturing activity—a position it continued to hold through 1970. During the war period the value of manufactured products tripled in comparison to what it had been in the thirties, so that by 1947 the figure reached $960 million. But the industrial boom of the 1950s and 1960s, stirred by the state government's recruitment of new industry and by TVA's abundant electricity and vastly improved river transportation system, caused the value added by manufacture to soar to almost $5 billion by 1967. Reflective of this spectacular growth were the corresponding increases in the number of industrial plants and workers. As always, industrialization hastened the movement of people to the cities. In 1930, one-third of all Tennessans were urban dwellers, but by 1970 the proportion had risen to 59 percent.

One unexpected and extraordinary economic development that came as a direct result of World War II was the creation of Oak Ridge, a totally new city. When Brigadier General Leslie R. Groves chose the Anderson County site in 1942, there was nothing there—precisely why he selected the location. Because of the availability of abundant cheap electricity and the isolated nature of the area, Groves and others reasoned that the site would be an excellent place to engage in the production of the uranium needed for the atomic bomb development. Shrouded in mystery and secrecy in the war years, Oak Ridge mushroomed from zero population to 50,000 inhabitants by 1944 and to a peak of 70,000 by 1945. Oak Ridge was thus an instant city, though it was at the same time a "frontier" in many respects, for it lacked most of the conveniences and facilities of cities of comparable size. Thousands of Tennesseans, as well as out-of-staters, found employment at the Oak Ridge project during the war, and their paychecks naturally had a positive impact upon the state's economy. When the war ended and the atomic bomb project concluded, Oak Ridge lost population rapidly and the new Atomic Energy

To keep pace with present and future energy needs in the state, TVA has constructed the Watts Bar Nuclear Plant, located near Spring City. Courtesy TVA.

Commission took over responsibility there. In the late 1940s Oak Ridge was opened to the public for the first time and the X-10 plant became the Oak Ridge National Laboratory. Union Carbide Corporation later began operating the Oak Ridge plants under contract with the federal government and in the late 1950s the city lost its unique status as an autonomous federal city within the state. By 1970 the population at Oak Ridge was 28,000—many of whom were still connected with atomic energy development and related concerns. Thus for decades now the research activities at Oak Ridge have attracted highly-trained individuals into the region and have boosted income levels of Anderson County and surrounding counties.

The unusual events of the thirties and the forties made their mark upon Tennessee's political life, much as they had done with the state's economic life. On the eve of the Great Depression, Governor Henry Horton, newspaper publisher Luke Lea, and businessman Rogers Caldwell seemed to constitute a three-man committee in charge of state government and politics. Bowing to this reality, Edward H. Crump, boss of Memphis, threw his support to Horton, when the governor sought reelection in 1930. A few days after Horton's success at the ballot boxes, however, came the shocking news that two of the Lea-Caldwell banks had collapsed—wiping out more than $6 million of state funds on deposit in those banks.

Crump immediately turned against the governor, declaring that the Lea-Caldwell scandal must be investigated and Horton impeached. In March 1931, a special legislative investigating committee recommended the governor's impeachment on charges of wrongdoing in connection with the banks and also with the highway department. But a full two months went by before the General Assembly took under consideration the committee's recommendation. Meanwhile, the governor and Luke Lea left no patronage stone unturned in their efforts to head off impeachment. Moreover, they launched a counterattack, laying all the blame for the impeachment furor at Crump's doorstep—a tactic designed to play upon rural leaders' fears of possible urban domination. By the time the legislature finally took a vote (in early June), the impeachment crusade had lost its momentum and Horton escaped this ultimate embarrassment. Although Horton remained in office for another year and a half, he was a largely discredited and ineffective governor.

For the moment Crump had lost the battle but perhaps not the war. In the 1932 gubernatorial contest, the Crump forces and the Horton-Lea axis faced a showdown, and Crump's candidate, State Treasurer Hill

McAlister squeaked by with victories in the Democratic primary and the general election. Shortly thereafter, Luke Lea went off to jail for some of his scandalous financial dealings and Crump assumed the role of boss of state politics. He proved repeatedly that he could make and break governors. Crump turned against McAlister in 1936, for example, and threw his support to Gordon Browning. But about a year after Browning's victory, Crump and the governor had a complete falling out. Crump therefore refused to support Browning's re-election bid in 1938, successfully backing Prentice Cooper instead.

During the war years and immediately thereafter, the political climate began to change. The Nashville *Tennessean* inaugurated a relentless attack upon Crump, mainly on the grounds that the state poll tax played into the hands of the Crump organization (since it reportedly paid the tax for many Shelby County voters). In response to the anti-poll tax sentiment throughout the state, the legislature repealed the tax in 1943, only to have the state supreme court declare the repeal invalid. Crump weathered that storm, but his luck and political strategies could not survive forever. In fact, five years later the Crump machine was dismantled by defeats in the 1948 presidential, gubernatorial, and Senate races. Crump, disliking the Democratic party's stance on civil rights that year, had bolted from the party to support the States Rights ticket in the presidential election. But then Truman, despite much unhappiness in Tennessee with him and his Democratic party, managed to carry the state by a small plurality. Meanwhile, in the governor's contest, Crump's old foe, Gordon Browning, gained delayed revenge by defeating the Crump candidate, James Nance McCord. Finally, in the U.S. Senate race, Crump's nemesis was a young Chattanooga congressman, Estes Kefauver, who sought the office. Crump, who mirrored post-war fears about international Communism, tried to smear Kefauver with the Communist sympathizer label, but he did not make believers out of many Tennesseans. Kefauver capitalized on the growing anti-Crump sentiment in the state, having recognized that post-war politics demanded new faces and the elimination of old bossism. Kefauver's success, linked with the presidential and gubernatorial contests, put the finishing touches on the Crump machine.

While Crump was in his heyday, dictating to governors and voters alike, another Tennessee political leader, Cordell Hull, was making news on the national and international fronts. With impressive credentials as a politician—chairman of the Democratic National Committee in the Republican decade of the 1920s and nearly twenty-five years in the U.S.

House and Senate—Hull had much to recommend him when Franklin Roosevelt became President in 1933. The new president needed a man in his cabinet who was wise to the ways of Capitol Hill and therefore turned to Hull, appointing him secretary of state. Throughout the Great Depression and most of World War II, Hull served in a quiet but highly effective way during eleven (1933–44) of the stormiest years any secretary of state has experienced. He achieved international recognition in the 1930s for his efforts to improve U.S. relations with the Latin American countries, but his last years in the cabinet were consumed by the global conflict among Germany, Japan, and the allied powers. During the war Hull pushed the idea that once the fighting ended, there must be an international organization for the maintenance of peace and security. His vision became reality in 1945 when at San Francisco the United Nations was born—the same year that Hull was awarded the Nobel Peace Prize, a fitting climax to his diligent efforts in behalf of world peace.

In the post-Crump years in Tennessee there was a movement toward the restoration of two-party politics and a resurgence of Republican strength. This trend was most immediately obvious in the presidential elections, for beginning in 1952 and continuing for the next twenty years Tennessee voted Republican in five of the six contests. The only deviation from the new pattern came in 1964, when the state went for Lyndon Johnson, the Democratic incumbent. But four years later Democratic strength had eroded so much that its candidate placed third in Tennessee, behind the Republican winner Richard M. Nixon and the American party contender George C. Wallace. These Republican victories did not necessarily mean that the state had abandoned the Democratic party, however, for it continued to dominate state and local elections.

But there were problems in the Democratic camp and they soon surfaced. Shortly after he became senator, Kefauver attracted national attention with his investigations of organized crime. This recognition catapulted him into new political realms, and Kefauver quickly took advantage of the situation by launching a folksy, homespun campaign for the presidential nomination in 1952. He stunned the experts first by winning the New Hampshire presidential primary and then by enlisting support in state after state. But at the convention, Kefauver lost out to Adlai Stevenson of Illinois. Four years later Kefauver once again en-

---

Ed Crump was a powerful Tennessee political boss for over forty years. Courtesy Memphis *Commercial Appeal.*

tered the presidential primaries and enjoyed some successes. When the party held its national convention, however, Kefauver bowed out of contention, letting Stevenson receive the nomination again. It was at this 1956 meeting that Governor Frank Clement delivered the keynote address, hoping to aid his own ambitions for national office; but things did not work out for him. Meanwhile Kefauver became interested in the vice-presidential nomination, only to discover that Senator Albert Gore was also mounting a campaign for convention votes. When the vice-presidential balloting began, both senators from Tennessee were in the race, putting Governor Clement and other Democratic leaders from Tennessee in a very uncomfortable position. Kefauver eventually won the spot on the ticket with Stevenson, and the party closed ranks for the campaign. But Eisenhower swept to another victory, in Tennessee and in the nation at large.

Upon the death of Kefauver in 1963, political bickering among Democrats grabbed the headlines. Governor Clement and Congressman Ross Bass fought over the Senate seat twice—Bass won it in 1964, but Clement defeated Bass two years later. The Democrats were so badly fragmented by the Clement-Bass feud, however, that in November 1966 Republican Howard Baker, Jr., defeated Clement and captured the Senate post. The divisiveness of the Democratic party continued to haunt it, helping make possible the defeat of Senator Gore by Republican William E. Brock in 1970 and the victory of Republican Winfield Dunn in the gubernatorial election that same year. Two-party rivalry was back in vogue in Tennessee—thanks to the political climate that had been changing over the preceding twenty years.

Another major area to feel the twin effects of the depression and the world war was public education, which in addition was pressured to take the lead in confronting the problem of racial segregation. State government took a decidedly negative attitude toward financing public schools in the difficult days of the 1930s. In fact, it required considerable effort on the part of education leaders to keep the legislature from closing down the teachers' colleges. They were kept open, but appropriations for higher education were slashed by two-thirds. Hopes for a state sales tax to provide new funding for public education were doomed once Edward H. Crump announced his opposition to such a tax. Pledges by governors in the 1930s to keep a balanced budget invariably worked against funding for public schools. Only as the state slowly began to recover from the devastating effects of the depression in the last year or two of the decade did the government loosen the purse strings a bit in behalf of education. The most important breakthrough for schools in Tennessee came in the mid-1940s, when Governor McCord began pushing the legislature for increased appropriations for education. The governor's urgings led to the enactment in 1947 of a sales tax, the revenue from which was designated for the support of education at all levels. Governors in the next two decades generally lent their power and influence to the cause of public schools, so that the educational system was saved from a nearly desperate condition. But Tennessee, like some other states, continued to strive to catch up with the needs left unattended in the decade of the 1930s.

Compounding the problems of government funding for schools was the decision, dating back to the 1870s, that Tennessee should maintain separate schools for blacks and whites. As a general rule, black schools suffered even more than did the white schools in the aftermath of the depression. Much of this disparity became evident in the 1950s when the dual system of education was challenged in Tennessee and elsewhere in the nation. When the United States Supreme Court ruled in *Brown v. Board of Education of Topeka* (1954) that segregated schooling was not constitutional, the time had arrived for Tennessee, and other states as well, to wrestle with the controversies of the dual system.

Racial conflict frequently accompanied the challenges to segregated schooling. Tennessee was unable to avoid such confrontations, which is not surprising if one remembers that racial antagonisms had been expressed overtly and sometimes violently in the decade prior to the desegregation difficulties. For example, as late as the 1940s lynchings of blacks occurred in Tennessee, and there were several flare-ups between black and white soldiers at the various military installations during World War II days. But Tennessee's worst example of racial violence took place in Middle Tennessee at Columbia in February 1946. The traditional lack of communication between the races was aggravated by the returning veterans, black and white, who harbored new fears and anxieties. These feelings spilled over into the community at large: whites feared the new militancy of some blacks, while blacks feared white recriminations against them for any break with custom and practice. The Columbia rioting was sparked by a fight between a white veteran and a black veteran. Eventually hundreds of both races were involved. Governor McCord sent in the state guard who finally brought an end to the hostilities, but not before two blacks had been killed and scores injured.

Ten years later the small number of blacks in Anderson County in East Tennessee protested against the absence of high school educational opportunities for their children. It had long been the practice there to bus black high school students to adjoining Knox County, while white students attended Clinton High School in Anderson County. A federal court order was issued, compelling the admission of black students at Clinton High. Things went smoothly at first as governmental and educational leaders made preparations for the registration of blacks in late August 1956. But at about the time of the opening of schools in Anderson County, John Kasper, an "outside agitator" from the Washington, D.C., area, arrived in Clinton. He immediately set about arousing the local citizenry to resist desegregation and succeeded in assembling an angry mob of pickets and protesters whose activities finally compelled Governor Clement to send in National Guard troops. Although the racial situation cooled down thereafter, a dynamite blast at the school the next year gave further evidence of the lingering anger and frustration in Anderson County.

In the summer of 1957 Nashville prepared to become the state's first major school system to desegregate. After much maneuvering by the city school board, actual desegregation was to involve only nineteen first-graders scattered among six different elementary schools. Although there was unhappiness and unease over even this very small-scale attack upon the traditional dual system, there was no indication of serious trouble until John Kasper arrived in Nashville in September. Much as in Clinton, Kasper rallied the segregationist forces in Nashville. After the first day of school ended, a dynamite explosion ripped through an elementary school attended by one black student. Although there was no evidence directly linking Kasper with that incident, police authorities quickly moved to arrest Kasper on various charges. The following year he began serving sentence in a federal prison for his activities at Clinton and Nashville. Nashville schools embarked upon a grade-a-year desegregation plan by the end of the decade. Soon other cities in the state began dismantling the segregated dual system.

Although there were sporadic difficulties as the school systems desegregated, no massive resistance to school desegregation developed, principally because Governors Frank Clement and Buford Ellington opposed such a movement. Even though subjected to much pressure from very vocal groups, Governor Clement did not bend. In fact he outflanked the segregationists by seeming to offer them legal havens in a package of five bills which he submitted to the legislature in 1957. In reality the bills constituted an innocuous collection of laws about school attendance and pupil assignment that were struck down by the courts subsequently.

Two years later Governor Ellington used a similar strategy when he promoted an ambiguous bill permitting parents to remove their children from the public schools for substantial reasons and with the permission of the local school board. This measure, passed by the legislature, was never carried out, and the law was so vague that not a single newspaper in the state commented upon it editorially. Both governors bought valuable time with their parliamentary activities so that they would not be pushed into actions that would heighten racial tensions over school desegregation. Never once did either governor boast about "standing in the schoolhouse door"—unlike governors in some other Southern states.

The desegregation of public schools in Tennessee was but the first sign heralding a new day of race relations in the state. Very shortly the quest for the dismantling of all vestiges of a racially segregated society moved from the classrooms to the streets. Throughout the decade of the 1960s, pickets, protest marches, sit-ins at lunch counters and movie houses, and other visible challenges to prevailing custom occurred. Slowly public transportation and public facilities—such as restaurants, theaters, and restrooms—were opened to members of both races. The federal government's involvement, especially with new voting rights legislation, assured blacks of an emerging role in the new society being created, but racial disturbances and violence nevertheless accompanied these breaks with tradition. Black-power advocate Stokely Carmichael introduced a threatening note of militancy to a white-dominated society, for instance, when his visit to Nashville in 1967 prompted turmoil and rioting in that city. And Martin Luther King, Jr., an Atlanta preacher who pushed for civil rights and social change on the basis of non-violent protests and who for more than ten years was the most renowned leader of black Southerners, was assassinated in Memphis in 1968. In bitter frustration over this shocking and traumatic event, blacks throughout the state took to the streets to vent their rage. Memphis had long been a strong segregationist center, but it probably did not deserve the stigma attached to it upon the death of King. Thankfully, when the decade ended, tangible signs of interracial progress abounded, although virtually everyone conceded that much more remained to be done.

In the 1950s and 1960s an extraordinary school in Tennessee helped develop leadership for the civil rights movement. Born in the depths of the depression of the 1930s, the Highlander Folk School had originally been interested in labor organizing and assistance to strikers at various scenes of labor disturbances. But in the period after World War II, the school became increasingly involved with the problems of blacks in the

South. The emerging black leaders of the region, not the least of whom was Martin Luther King, Jr., went to Highlander for instruction and inspiration.

With the heating up of racial tensions in the late 1950s the General Assembly decided to launch an investigation of the Highlander School. Although eagerly searching for evidence of subversion and Communist sympathies at Highlander, the special legislative committee found none. Nevertheless it recommended that the state revoke the school's charter. The mounting attack upon Highlander reached its climax with a raid upon the school conducted by state and county officials in August 1959. The following year, the lower courts as well as the state supreme court agreed to revoke Highlander's charter. But as the school's founder, Myles Horton, told the courts, they could not put Highlander out of business because it was more than a mere school; it was an idea.

When state officials shut down the Highlander School, then in Grundy County, Horton applied for a new charter from the state which was rather routinely granted. Horton then moved his school to Knoxville, where it continued to face hostility and harassment from certain local leaders for the next ten years. But the school persisted in its promotion of the civil rights crusade until 1972, when it moved to the vicinity of New Market in Jefferson County and redirected its focus to the Appalachian poor, black and white.

The racial struggles of the fifties and sixties in the schools, courts, and streets served as a pointed reminder that even in the midst of sweeping change in the twentieth century, old attitudes and customs remained. But on the other hand, the victories won by black Tennesseans were further indication of how much the experiences of the Great Depression and World War II had shaped and altered society. And those who think back to the earlier days of this century will be tremendously impressed, nearly overwhelmed, by the breadth and depth of the changes wrought in the lives of all Tennesseans. There remains nevertheless the lingering notion that some things do not change—an idea reinforced by present-day urgings of the proponents of a return to the old ways: natural foods, hand crafts, less dependence upon modern appliances, the three R's in school, and in general, more self-sufficiency. The immensely complex, complicated society, so it is argued, must be overcome by recapturing the simple life. Small wonder then that one might feel compelled to think of Tennessee in the twentieth century as a fascinating amalgam of something old, something new.

Selected Readings

It is very easy to resist the temptation to supply an extensive list of books on various aspects of Tennessee history, mainly because there already exists an excellent bibliography, edited and compiled by Sam B. Smith, *Tennessee History: A Bibliography* (1974). Smith's monumental work is exhaustive and comprehensive and contains entries of books and articles published prior to the end of 1972. All persons interested in pursuing some topic in Tennessee history should first consult the Smith bibliography for leads to pertinent materials.

For scholarly articles relative to Tennessee that have appeared since 1972, one should examine the issues of the *Tennessee Historical Quarterly,* the East Tennessee Historical Society's *Publications* and the West Tennessee Historical Society *Papers.* These three journals are the principal sources of essays on Tennessee history, although occasionally the *Journal of Southern History* has articles with an exclusive Tennessee focus.

Readers wanting a one-volume history of Tennessee would be well advised to acquire *Tennessee, A Short History* (1969) by Stanley J. Folmsbee, Robert E. Corlew, and Enoch L. Mitchell, which despite its title is over 600 pages in length. Essentially a college textbook, this work has a relatively complete bibliography that has been superseded, of course, by the Smith book. Individuals desiring a much more compact version of Tennessee history should see Wilma Dykeman, *Tennessee: A Bicentennial History* (1975), a selective and very readable 200-page history.

Since 1972, Tennessee has been enriched by the appearance of a number of monographs which have added new information and understanding about the state's past. Three works, not dealing solely with Tennessee but containing valuable material relevant to the state are: Ralph A. Wooster, *Politicians, Planters, and Plain Folk: Courthouse and Statehouse in the Upper South, 1850–1860* (1975), Neal R. Peirce, *The Border South States: People, Politics, and Power in the Five States of the*

Border South (1975), and Blaine A. Brownell, *The Urban Ethos in the South, 1920–1930* (1975). In the latter study Memphis, Nashville, and Knoxville are among the seven cities of the central South examined by Brownell.

In the past few years university presses have published several very fine studies that treat Tennessee in the latter half of the nineteenth century and the early twentieth century. These include: James L. McDonough, *Shiloh—in Hell before Night* (1977), Robert B. Jones, *Tennessee at the Crossroads: The State Debt Controversy, 1870–1883* (1977), Roger L. Hart, *Redeemers, Bourbons, & Populists: Tennessee, 1870–1896* (1975), and Joseph H. Cartwright, *The Triumph of Jim Crow: Tennessee Race Relations in the 1880s* (1976). The major scholarly monograph pertinent to twentieth-century Tennessee that has appeared recently is Lester C. Lamon, *Black Tennesseans, 1900–1930* (1977).

Among the books about local areas that have been published since 1972 are: J. Leonard Raulston and James W. Livingood, *Sequatchie: A Story of the Southern Cumberlands* (1974) and a study of the Little Tennessee River region by Alberta and Carson Brewer, *Valley So Wild: A Folk History* (1975). New editions of books published earlier have appeared recently: Betsey Beeler Creekmore, *Knoxville* (3d ed., 1976) and Gilbert E. Govan and James W. Livingood, *The Chattanooga Country 1540–1976: From Tomahawks to TVA* (3d ed., 1977). A new compilation of essays on Knoxville was published in 1976, *Heart of the Valley: A History of Knoxville, Tennessee,* edited by Lucile Deaderick. Several pictorial histories of various Tennessee towns and cities have also appeared within the past five years.

The Tennessee American Revolution Bicentennial Commission published several informative and attractive booklets that are of interest to students of the state's history. The two that appeared in 1976 were: Robert E. Corlew, *Statehood for Tennessee* and Max Dixon, *The Wataugans.* Published in 1977 were: Edward Michael McCormack, *Slavery on the Tennessee Frontier;* Muriel Spoden, *The Long Island of the Holston;* and James C. Kelly, *From Settlement to Statehood: A Pictorial History of Tennessee to 1796.*

This brief list of additional books on Tennessee history is not intended to be complete or even totally representative of all that has been published since 1972 about Tennessee, for I have been quite selective. But it is hoped that this sampling conveys something of the variety and richness of the newer publications.

Index

Tennessee Three Star Books

Visions of Utopia
Nashoba, Rugby, Ruskin, and the "New Communities" in Tennessee's Past
by John Egerton

Our Restless Earth
The Geologic Regions of Tennessee
by Edward T. Luther

Tennessee Strings
The Story of Country Music in Tennessee
by Charles K. Wolfe

Paths of the Past
Tennessee, 1770–1970
by Paul H. Bergeron

Civil War Tennessee
Battles and Leaders
by Thomas L. Connelly

Tennessee's Indian Peoples
From White Contact to Removal, 1540–1840
by Ronald N. Satz

Blacks in Tennessee, 1791–1970
by Lester C. Lamon

Religion in Tennessee, 1777–1945
by Herman A. Norton

Tennessee Writers
by Thomas Daniel Young

Tennessee's Presidents
by Frank B. Williams, Jr.

THE UNIVERSITY OF TENNESSEE PRESS
KNOXVILLE 37996-0325